The Amazing John Heigham Steggall, 'The Suffolk Gipsy'

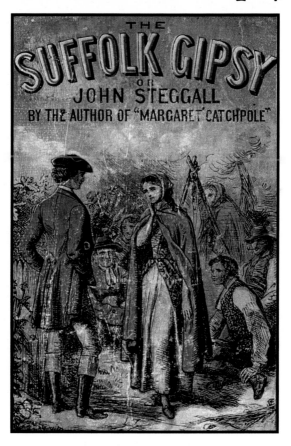

revised and researched
by Pip & Joy Wright

Published by **Pawprint Publishing**
14, Polstead Close, Stowmarket, Suffolk   IP14 2PJ

Thanks and acknowledgement are due to a number of people
without whose help, the publication of this book would not have
been possible. These include the staff at the Suffolk Record
Offices at Ipswich and Bury St. Edmunds;
the Norfolk Millennium Library;
the librarians at Corpus Christi College;
also, Jean Folkard, James Turner, Keith Robathan,
Dr. E. Cockayne, Jean Wallwork, Mrs. P. Bell,
Sharon Foate, Dr. A. Wankowski, Gordon Boswell,
Cro Page and various members of the Seeley family.

Front cover design by **Daniel Wright**

Printed by **Polstead Press**, Station Rd. East, Stowmarket,
Suffolk IP14 1RQ
First reprint July 2006
Second January 2008

In the Autumn of 1854, *'a venerable gentleman'** called at Wortham Rectory near Diss. He was an elderly curate who had driven himself in a pony gig from Great Ashfield where he lived and ministered. He was calling on the Reverend Richard Cobbold, rector of Wortham and a well-known and respected writer. What transpired from this meeting was the publishing of a book: **'John H. Steggall, a real history of a Suffolk Man,'** the autobiography of a man who had been a gipsy, a sailor, a soldier, a surgeon and finally a clergyman.

Wortham Rectory

This story was published a number of times during the second half of the nineteenth century, eventually having the title *'The Suffolk Gipsy.'* When we came across this book, it fascinated and intrigued us - was it a true story or the result of an active imagination? What concerned us most was Richard Cobbold's role in the enterprise. As editor, how much was his work and just how much belonged to the story of John Heigham Steggall? Cobbold's books are still read to this day, but are well known for their rather romanticised versions of real events.

*The words of Richard Cobbold himself in the book's introduction

Rev. Richard Cobbold

Richard Cobbold had written a number of books including a best-seller about Margaret Catchpole, which, although based on a true story, deviated wildly from the facts.

Using such evidence as still remains, alongside an edited and somewhat reduced version of Steggall's original text, we have tried to uncover the truth behind the remarkable story of John Heigham Steggall.

John Heigham Steggall as pictured in the first edition of the book

Hoping it is not too disruptive to the reader, we have inserted shaded boxes from time to time that seek to clarify, as the story unravels, some of the evidence we have been able to find in support of John Steggall's amazing tale. We should explain, the original is a rambling book and we have judiciously removed sections of text that seem superfluous to the plot. What remains is a remarkable autobiography, which does not always tally with the facts as they appear to us. For all that, a great deal of 'The Suffolk Gipsy' can be shown to be true.

So what is it safe to believe and what should we distrust? Read on...

The Amazing Story of
John Heigham Steggall, 'The Suffolk Gipsy'

Chapter 1 ~ Early Life

Life, it may be truly said, has its ups and downs with all men. Even those who are born to affluence are born to trouble as other people, and are not free from the cares incident to human nature. The following narrative may be depended upon as not fictitious, but as indicative of the strange feelings which an all-wise Providence pursues to bring about his own purposes, until he ends all things with us and brings us to himself.

I was born of respectable parents, in that pleasant little town called Needham Market, in the county of Suffolk, in the year 1789.

The baptism register for Creeting St. Mary, near Needham Market contains the following entry: *Steggall - John son of Charles Steggall & Mary his wife (late Mary Steggall Spinster) was born May ye 8th 1791. Privately baptized. May 9th 1791, Received into the Church.* This would have been much closer to the date of his birth than the 1789 he quotes in his story. Private baptisms were usually carried out if there was a fear that the child was weak and might not live to be christened in a church. Often, these private baptisms were carried out by midwives or doctors, but in this case Charles Steggall probably baptised his own child.

My father, like many thousand others at that period, had just sufficient competency to keep the respectable appearance of a gentleman without taking any prominent part either in the public matters of the county, or in the more immediate duties of the district. In fact, my father was neither a country squire nor magistrate, nor sufficiently rich or consequential to thrust himself into notice, but contented himself in living upon his income, and as a country clergyman performing the duties of Barham House, Needham Market. In fact, he was a country curate, not as yet come into his livings of Westhorpe and Wyverstone, held by his father before him.

St. George's Church, Wyverstone

Still, though my father was a gentleman by birth, he had not always been inactive, but had three duties to perform, which are now divided and shared by three different clergymen.

It can be seen from the family tree at the end of this book that the Steggall family spawned a number of clergymen. As rector of Wyverstone from 1794, and of Westhorpe from 1812, John Steggall's father, Charles, would have earned in excess of £600 per annum. John's grandfather, William, having the income from three rectories, would have earned rather more.

William Steggall died in 1794, allowing his son, Charles, to take on the 'preferment' of Wyverstone. John Heigham Steggall would not be so fortunate.

The Steggalls would have regarded themselves as a family of substance. They were linked to the Le Grys family, whose genealogy can be traced back to the time of the Conqueror.

My mother was a most notable person: an excellent housekeeper, an excellent mother, and an excellent wife. She might be termed homely, because she was almost always at home, and gave her lord and master as little occasion ever to find fault as one of the most conscientious women could do. She was scrupulously exact, and never gave way to any of that sentimental tenderness called romance. There was nothing of the sort in her. Her reading for her day was confined to scripture, and the history of her own country. She had no accomplishments beyond the use of her needle and her bodkin; and when my father, who was rather fond of books, used now and then to indulge her with a play of Shakespeare, she used to say, in her quaint way, "All very well; but nothing but fancy!"

I had one brother and two sisters, viz., William Charles, and Marian and Margaret. I was the youngest, John, and, consequently, it fell to my lot to take the latest departure from the paternal roof, to be qualified for any situation which my father might consider he could place me in.

There was a Grammar School at Needham Market, at which sixteen or seventeen free boys were educated, belonging to Needham Market, Darmsden and Barking; but my father was considered too wealthy a man to have me admitted therein; consequently, I was sent to a school, then considered a good one, and in much repute - namely, that of Mr. Edmund Rogers, of Walsham-le-Willows, where, with some fifty or sixty youths, the sons of gentlemen and tradesmen, I at seven years of age first took up my abode.

Terror was the system under which we were all trained. The mind of a boy in that day was not considered in the light of a rational or religious character, or as to be taught anything with a view to any future action in life, but solely according to the prospect of temporal possessions, and for one and all the same form was pursued, the same lessons exacted, and the treatment of all dispositions was exactly alike.

We have tried hard to place Mr Edmund Rogers' boys' school which must have lain somewhere along the Finningham Road leading out of Walsham. Two possibilities have come to light, and it is impossible to rule out either. These are the large houses known today as *The Rookery* and *Woodlands*. For reasons that are to follow, we favour *The Woodlands*. It was surrounded by a wall and had ample room to house the fifty or sixty boys, not all of whom would have been boarders.

The Rookery - some modern hearsay evidence places Edmund Rogers' boys' school here, though the case for *The Woodlands* seems stronger.

Woe be to either the tender-hearted or fond boy, who leaves the parental roof, where warm affections existed, and the encouraging smiles from a tender mother or sisters could call forth similar regard - when he has, as I had, to be placed under the tuition and care of such a master as Mr. Edmund Rogers.

8

Edmund Rogers and his wife, Frances, ran *'a respectable boarding school'* in Walsham from the early 1760s. On his death at the age of 74 in January 1807, the Bury Post included an obituary that portrayed him in a rather different light from Steggall's book. The Ipswich Journal for that month included the following lines: *Yesterday se'nnight died in the 74th year of his age, after a severe illness which he supported with Christian fortitude, Mr. Edmund Rogers, who kept the respectable boarding school at Walsham le Willows 46 years. He possessed a truly benevolent heart, and for uprightness and integrity in every transaction of life was exemplary.*
In an obituary to Mrs. Rogers, who died a year later, their school was described as a girls' school.

Several newspaper adverts appeared, relating to schools run by Edmund and Frances Rogers. One advertisement in the Bury Post in January 1787 referred to a school for young ladies. It is known from surviving documents that they had a girls' school at 'The Rosary' in Walsham. However, other adverts made no mention of the sex of children attending.

Within a few months of their father's death in 1807, his son Arthur, and one of his daughters, Rebecca, opened separate schools in Walsham and Botesdale, placing adverts in the Bury Post and Ipswich Journal. Both solicited a continuance of the favours afforded to their parents. However, it is significant that several of Arthur Rogers' advertisements refer to the education of *'young gentlemen.'* It would not seem unreasonable to suggest that he was continuing with one of a pair of schools that his parents had formerly run.

Arthur was rector of Sapiston. With his wife, he had already run a school at Chelmsford. Rebecca Rogers married the Rev. William Haddock later that year. Her elder sister, Frances had already married the Rev. John Spring Casborne of Pakenham.

Prior to the transfer of schools from Edmund & Frances Rogers to their children, an auction was held to sell all their effects, which included 30 feather beds.

In these days boys are trained to love good instruction, and beneath the quiet patience of calm dignity, not to be afraid to learn. In that day it was - "go and do it" - "find out yourself how it is to be done," and, if not done well, the doing soon became worse, because of the trembling hand, the terrified spirit, and the awful punishment of the "patter," the rod, and the whip, which were very soon applied, sans ceremonie, and without any power of redress.

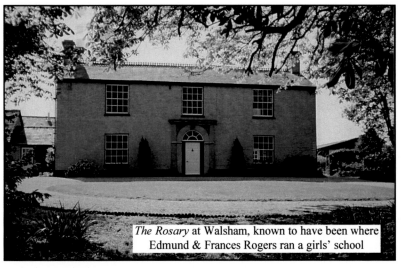

The Rosary at Walsham, known to have been where
Edmund & Frances Rogers ran a girls' school

I had not been in the school seven days before, for a simple deficiency in the multiplication of the number seven, I was severely whipped, and breeched as though I were guilty of some crime. I am quite certain that no parent who loved his child could have resisted the impulse to retaliate upon such a master, who had about as much feeling for a boy as a game-keeper has for a pointer puppy. I dreaded him beyond anything tongue can express. Fancy a young boy of seven held on the back of another boy, flogged till the blood span out of him, and only because of a mistake in his multiplication table, and which neither tears nor entreaties could avert.

We feel that even if nothing else in this book is true, this part of the story clearly is. A bitterness comes through his writing that seems to have remained with him for over fifty years. There are plenty of characters in this book whose names have been changed or disguised - not so Edmund Rogers.

The Woodlands

The Woodlands is a substantial 15th century house on the Finningham Road. Everything about it seems right regarding it being the site of Edmund Rogers' boys' school. Surrounded by a low wall, anyone leaving the propery would find *'the rippling village stream'* beside him as he went up through Walsham village. The Woodlands has a vast loft-space, plastered and oak-boarded, once having had a number of roof lights, now tiled over. The present owner has found in the loft space remains of old toys, and notes from mothers to their sons. Unfortunately, the surviving deeds offer no evidence that Edmund Rogers once had the property, though it was common for places to be let and sub-let, in a way that left little paperwork to show who had actually been in possession of the property at a given moment in time.

In the loft at *The Woodlands*, it is still possible to see what may have been the boys' dormitories. The oak boarding and plastered walls remain, though most of the roof windows have now gone.

Though the house became a school again in the early 20th century, the loft spaces were not used.

Assuredly, there appeared to me to be neither mind, mercy, nor justice in such a man; and the consequence was, that he never made a scholar, though he gained sufficient money to live and die in affluence.

My father was a strict disciplinarian; and when he did exercise the rod of correction, it was either for some fault of which my mother complained, or to uphold the authority of the master, under whose care I was placed, so that though I ran away from school once, and fled from the cruelty of the oppressor, to the home where I expected justice, judgement, and mercy to abide, yet I was represented as a refractory spirit, which required the strongest measures of coercion to restrain. I was sent back - I was publicly disgraced - I was flogged - and though for a time

I was degraded and reduced to the spirit of a slave and a dog, who had constantly to mind the master's eye, I never got a dog's caress, but was always treated with harshness.

I can only say, that the treatment I received was such that my spirit could not bear it. In short, one night I crept from my bed-fellow's side, and managed to descend the staircase unheard; slowly unbolted the school door, climbed over the playground wall, and made away from the school of Mr. Rogers of Walsham-in-the-Willows. The night was a bright one; and it was about a month before the mid-summer holidays. I knew it was in vain to seek a home beneath my father's roof, though he had now come into his living, and I, as such was the case, had no home to go to; I knew not my heart's home. I knew but one joy, that I had escaped from tyrannical treatment and oppression, and I was resolved to get away from such a place, and to take my chance in the wide world, wherever I could find anything to do.

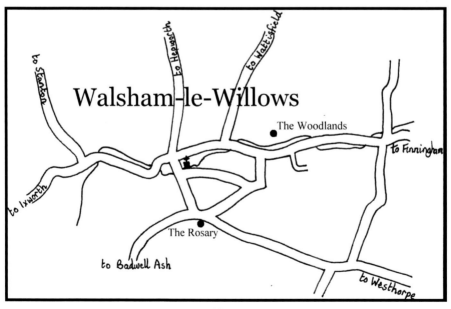

I had good, robust health. I was between eight and nine years old, of a lively, cheerful, active, and obliging nature, and I was not addicted at that time to any one vice. I hated quarrelling, and was fond of reading poetry, and of games of play, and of nick-nacks, jumping, skipping, and such amusements as boys of a lively spirit generally enjoy. But I went sorrowfully along through the pretty village of Walsham, hearing only the rippling village stream, where the water ran through many archways, and the cats fighting on the roofs of the cottages.

Walsham-le-Willows

My object was to hide myself up in some wood, until all pursuit should fail, to beg a piece of bread of anyone, and to drink of any stream that I might find. As I crept along through the village of Badwell Ash, and the light of morning began to dawn, and the birds to twitter, as if talking to each other, I could not help thinking I had no one to speak to me, no one to care about me, and that I was a poor, lone, weary boy, who had not even a brother to gather blackberries with, and to love me, like the babes in the wood, of whom we read in the nursery tales.

Little did I think, as I ought to have done, of the providential care that was over me. Little did I think that my heart would ever be cheered by human kindness; and least of all did I suppose that I should find a habitation, and brothers and sisters, in that very lane upon which I was then entering. But so it was.

Just as I was approaching the Hundred Lane, as it was called, in the parish of Wyverstone, I met a tall, gaunt-looking figure, which said to me in a gruff voice, "Boy, what do you here?"

Once, the Hundred Lane would have been an important routeway. Today, it is overgrown, but is still impressive, seen as a raised mound between ditches, cutting its way across the open landscape.

This Hundred Lane divided the ancient hundreds of Hartismere to the East and Blackbourn to the West. It was also the boundary between the parishes of Westhorpe & Walsham-le-Willows and Wyverstone & Badwell Ash.

Now it was very true in my case, that the 'empty traveller fears not the robber', and though I had often heard of such men, even then, as Dick Turpin, yet I had brains enough to know that Dick, or such as he, would not rob a beggar boy, so I simply said in reply, "Nothing."

"Doing nothing, young one," said the man; "doing nothing? Don't tell me; you are after catching some of Sir George Wombwell's hares. Who employs you?"

Sir George Wombwell was a leading landowner in the area at the time. He is not to be confused with the showman and menagerie-owner of the same name.

I supposing him, then, to be a gamekeeper, said to him, "No, I am not, I am no poacher."

How quick is the penetration of the man who has to live by his wits. That man knew by the sound of my voice, by the words I uttered, and by my tone of speech, all about me, for he said: "Young one, you have run away from home. You are not a poor man's child. You have met with cruel treatment, and you don't care what becomes of you."

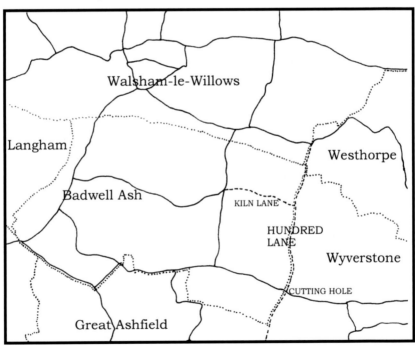

I maintain, in the face of all men, that the man who so accosted me was a clever fellow, for it was yet so dark that we could neither of us see each other's faces plainly, and yet that man had wit, or wisdom, or penetration enough to know my history in a moment, only from the tone of my voice.

I burst into tears; I sobbed aloud; for my heart owned that there was something almost supernatural in the person who accosted me, and I felt that he had spoken the truth.

"Come boy, come, cheer up! I dare say you are hungry; come along with me. Do not be afraid, I will not hurt you. Come along, come along." And with that, he took my trembling hand in his, and led me along the lane, until we reached a gipsies' encampment, when, giving a whistle, there came peeping out of a low tent hard by, a boy and girl, to whom he said something in a language I could not then comprehend, but which I took to be of this nature:

"Here, Jack, take this younker in; give him something to eat, and be kind to him."

For the first time in my life I found myself seated in a gipsies' tent. It was warm and pleasant to the poor wanderer, and truly, being an object of their sympathy, I thought them the kindest-hearted creatures I had ever met with.

The two who took me in introduced me to two others, for they soon struck a light, lit a little straw, opened a little fissure at the end of the tent, so that the smoke was driven out at the entrance, and they kindly seated me on the windward side of the smoke, which, notwithstanding that it made my eyes water, did not stop the genuine tears which came from my heart.

"Come, don't cry," said the swarthy, half-dressed maiden. "We won't rob you, we won't ill treat you, we will restore you to your friends - don't cry, don't cry."

This made me cry the more heartily, and but that I dare not, I verily believe I could have kissed my swarthy sister, and have blessed her for her goodness.

They were very kind to me. Oh what a contrast! Oh what a lesson! These offcasts from society, these children of Cain, these deserted, houseless wanderers, received with kindness the son of a gentleman, and made him feel more at home and more happy than he had felt since he had left his good mother's roof to dwell with Mr. Edmund Rogers, of Walsham-in-the-Willows, the unkind and irritable schoolmaster.

"Tell us now who you are," said one of those in the tent.

I told them all my story, and as I narrated to them my daily floggings, I could see the blood boil beneath their dark skins, and if revenge had been in me, I am confident I could then have induced them to take summary vengeance on the schoolmaster. But I was too joyous to have escaped, too happy not to show it in my countenance, and too grateful to them for their kindness not to touch their hearts with pity.

At no period of my life do I ever remember being so kindly treated as among these strangers. Had I been a prince I could not have received more devoted affection, and if ever in after life I met with gipsies, I never forgot, and never can forget, the native dignity of that protection, which, in the hour of my distress, these proscribed vagabonds, as they were termed, exhibited towards me. I was happy, very happy. I was but a poor, tender, broken-hearted boy, so ill-treated as to run away from all my relatives, and then took up my abode among the gipsies. Fancy a boy eight years old having experienced such decided inhumanity, if I may so term it, as to be compelled to flee from the most monstrous unkind treatment, and then to find himself a welcome guest among the poorest of the poor.

To describe my abode among the gipsies would fill volumes. My first day among them was one of interest and anxiety. Interest, because of the interest they took in me; and fear, less they should betray me under the idea of doing me good.

"Keep you quiet within the tent all this day," said the old man, "and, if you want a job, take that knife, and my girl there will show you how to peel those willows in the corner, and to split them afterwards; and if, as I suspect, you are not quite good for nothing, she will teach you in a little time how to make a basket."

This was both wise and kind: wise, because it first gave me the idea that I could be of any service, and was not quite good for nothing, and kind, because it found me an easy employment, and prevented those fears which every fugitive naturally feels for some time before he is quite reconciled to his new condition.

19

A basket weaver

I went heartily to work to peel the long strips of willow bark from their stems, and positively I went at it so heartily and steadily that when the mother of the gipsies came in, and learnt from her youngest boy and eldest girl that I had peeled such a bundle, she gave me a kiss of approbation which again made me cry. Oh it was so pleasant! It was gratifying to have and to hear those words, "Well done, well done!"

About noon Jack came into the tent, having wandered with a basket upon a begging expedition into the parish of Walsham.

"Well, younker, you have created a fine hubbub in the parish of Walsham. Some say you have drowned yourself. Some say that you have run home. Some say you were seen against Hunt's pond; and one old woman declared that you were running like a mad-dog across the lands towards Ixworth. Your old master, Rogers, I saw myself speaking to the constable of the parish, and I heard him say, 'I dare say the young dog has gone home, but let him be gone where he will; he is a good-for-nothing young scamp, and when he comes back I will make an example of him. I'll flay him alive.'"

"I hope he will not find me," was my reply, and I looked round the little tent very wistfully to see if there was any place in which, in case of alarm, I could be hidden. They saw my perturbation and smiled.

Weary travellers resting beside the Hundred Lane

Presently, in came the tall father of the family, creeping upon his hands and knees, and quite unable to sit up in the tent; but, reclining his head upon the bundle of bed-clothes rolled up at one end, and his feet reaching nearly to the door, he looked at me with some interest.

"Young lad," he said, "do you wish to be restored to your friends?"

"Not yet," said I.

"Humph!" was the old man's expression; as if he thought that I should one day leave him of my own accord.

"How long would you like to live here?"

"As long as you are kind to me," said I.

"Humph!" again.

"Did you peel those sticks yourself?"

"Yes, father, he did," said the girl.

"Who asked you that question, Mog? I asked the boy."

"Yes, I did, but Mog taught me."

"You have worked well, but if you wish to remain here you must be a gipsy, or at least look more like one than you now do. There is a reward of a guinea offered to any one who will bring you in."

"Pray don't take me back," said I; "Pray don't take me back!"

"I was not going to do so; but you must take those things off your back, or you will very soon be carried back, for I expect there will be some country fellows in search of you soon, who would like to have a guinea in their hands, and have us gipsies sent to gaol for kidnapping you."

"Pray take my clothes; pray lend me some others; and do what you will with me, only do not let me fall into the grasp of that same tyrant again."

"Jack, get one of Barnaby's begging suits, and doff the youngster's blue jacket. Mog, get your mother's shears and just cut off those curly locks of the young gentleman. Jin go you and bring out of your mother's tent some of the boiled willow peelings which have been burnt and seething there since the morning, and give him a regular wash."

So did the gipsy presently employ all his family to disguise me. I was soon stripped, washed, clipped, and dressed, and actually one of the girls went and fetched a piece of broken looking glass, and showing me myself therein, made me have such a fit of laughter that even the long, lank, grim, and greasy-looking gipsy could not help joining in the laugh. I certainly never beheld such a thorough blackguard-looking young lad as I was made to look in five minutes.

My fair face was as sallow as if I had been smoked for a month; my teeth were white; my eyes, which were hazel, were now surrounded by such dark eyelids, that positively I had no idea that I could have been so speedily transmogrified. All the ringlets were shorn from my hair, and Mog had so sheared and stiffened it, that there I was, worse than any union boy with his hair polled, and thoroughly transformed. As to my dress, oh ye mothers who love the decency of your darlings, I had a dried sheepskin jacket, which served me for a waistcoat and coat; a pair of trousers, made of the old smoky tent tarpaulin; no stockings; no gloves; no hat but a greasy old dog's-skin or cat's-skin cap; in fact, I was a young vagabond in appearance, and though not yet a vagabond in heart, I might very easily be thought one.

"They will never know him, father, never."

"Give me his clothes, Mog."

They were done up in a bundle, and in a very curious place were they deposited. A square piece of turf was taken up in the tent - which had evidently been removed and put down before - and underneath that turf there was a large boiler with a top to it, which being taken off, my bundle of gentleman's clothes was thrust without ceremony into it, my hat crushed to a pancake. The lid of the pot was put on again, the turf covered over it, and sticks, and pots, and pans laid thereon, so that no one could have possibly conceived such a gipsy's cup-board, unless they had experienced, as I then did, the use of it.

"Now boy," said the gipsy, "you must learn to act, if you can, and pretend to be deaf and dumb, and not to see or know anything. If any one should come into our tent - as you may depend upon it they will before the day is past - you must take no notice of any one; stare at the smoke, and sit with your hands upon your knees like a fool; or you may do that which appears to suit you better, go on peeling the sticks."

I am quite sure that I learned this lesson of deception quicker than I learned any other lesson at school, all the days I was at Mr. Rogers' Academy, and it was very necessary that I should be an apt scholar, for I was very soon put to the test.

"Hullo, Jim! Who is that coming up the lane?"

"Why, that's the constable of the parish of Walsham,

along with Fake the carpenter. You may depend upon it we shall have a search. Now, young one, sit you at your sticks."

According to directories from a time shortly after, and parish records of the time, the 'Fake' family were carpenters and wheelwrights at Badwell Ash

"Hullo! Hullo! Master Gibson, we want to have a word with you."

This was the first time I had heard the name of the gipsy - Gibson, Master Gibson - so thinks I, I must be a Gibson.   I could hear the conversation, and Mog sat peering into my face to see how I took it.

"Who have you got there in your tent, Master Gibson? We are bound to look for a young gentleman, who has run away from school at Walsham, and is suspected of being with you, and that you are harbouring him in your tent."

"Go in if you like, and look."

"We don't want to go in; but have you anybody there?"

"Yes: I've poor Tom, the idiot, deaf and dumb; Mog, my daughter; and Jin, my youngest.   You met my boys, Jack and Barnaby, and I hope you didn't find anything wrong.   Pray look in."

I saw two heads stare in, and Mog and I kept on peeling the willow sticks, and as innocently as possible.

"What do you see, Master Fake?"

"I can see two or three urchins peeling sticks, that's all.   But we are bound to search!   Perhaps you'll order your fry to come forth!"

"Oh, yes.   Mog, come out; Jin, come out.   Take care of your brother."

We all came out. I grinning, and staring in the face of the constable of Walsham, whom I knew as well as I did old Rogers; for he, as constable, questman, and sexton,

24

used to keep boys quiet at church, dig graves, and carry persons to prison, all in the course of due authority.

"The young lad missing is just the size of this boy of yours."

I stared in his face, as if I did not know what he said.

"He has a wild eye - curly hair - sharp look - is very strong for such a lad - and just this boy's height."

Certainly, I did not look very bright; I had no longer curly locks; I might have a wild eye, but though my mind was not in the least degree a vacant one, yet it looked, I suspect, wild enough at the constable; but I lifted up the stick, put my long, browned fingers to the top of it, and drew off such a long strip of green and yellow peel, and grinned at it so beautifully, that the old constable could not help saying, "Poor boy! He must be a sad misfortune to you, Master Gibson. I hope you are kind to him."

Mog patted me on the head. I knew, of course, what was said, and I looked at her, and laughed so pleased, that Mog herself could not help smiling at the artful dodge of my young idiocy.

"Here, poor boy, here's a penny for you!" said the constable.

But I was deaf - I could not hear. It was the first time I would not hear, and it would have been a good thing indeed if I had not heard many more enticing things than this first offer of a penny.

"He's quite deaf, Mr. Fake."

"And quite dumb, too?"

"Poor boy! I did not know you had such an affliction. We'll just look into the tents."

They did so, and found nothing. When they came out the constable said to the gipsy, "There's a guinea reward offered for the apprehension or capture of the younker; and if, in your wanderings, you should find him, a guinea, Master Gibson, is worth the handling."

"Pray, do you want any baskets, Sir?" said Mog. "Any tea kettles mending - any wooden bowls, Sir? Poor Tom, here, can make many things, and works hard, though he is an idiot boy."

And she gave me a look so knowing, that I understood how completely the constables were gulled, and what an apt scholar I had become at deception. The Gibsons were all clever gipsies, and, to a certainty, they made me quickly as clever as themselves. The constables departed, and we had a bolt into the tent, and a roar of fun and laughter at the acting.

This picture from a somewhat later time shows the gipsy tents which had changed little in hundreds of years. It also shows what we refer to as a gipsy caravan, the like of which would not have been made until the 1870s.

Chapter 2 ~ Gipsy Life

To describe my gipsy life would fill many a volume, though the incidents were of a character as yet unknown to society. I was witness, in this family of the Gibsons, to a decorum and a respect from every member of it, such as I never shall forget. I did not lie down that night in the midst of school fellows, who were curious to look at my scars, nor with a heart heavy with the consciousness of cruelty, with the sensitive suffering of a degraded boy. No; I felt for the first time that I had acted my part well, though it was one of cleverness beyond the mere repetition of a lesson. Certainly these gipsies were all my friends; and why? Because I had thrown myself on no other feeling than their pity for protection. They had hid me, fed me, housed me, when I was a wanderer, and I felt grateful to them then, and do so to this day.

My first supper was not a bad one, though I had no pinafore, no slap of the head for not sitting still, and no disgusting or unkind reproach for having too great an appetite. We had chicken broth for supper - dinner was out of the question. The gipsies' grand meal is supper; and the preparation of it and for it are equally matters of delight.

'The Higgler'
by Harry Becker

Outside our encampment, which consisted only of three tents - one for the master and his wife, and one for the boys, and another for the girls - we all had our supper in the open air in the summer evenings; and never shall I forget seeing the one iron cauldron boiling on a fire of sticks, constantly fed, stick by stick, not in large quantities, but with just enough fuel to keep a gentle flame constantly at the bottom of the cauldron. I say, I never shall forget the marked kindness paid to me; for whilst all the family of children had but one wooden bowl to eat out of, I had as neat a pipkin presented to me as any child could possibly desire. I am not persuaded that it was not bought for me that very day. It was bright, clean, and handsome in my eyes, and a complete contrast to my own dirty self, in my sheepskin and tarpaulin trousers.

We had chicken broth. It might be an old hen given to the gipsy in exchange for a tin pan, or it might be stolen, but of that, of course, I knew nothing; all I knew was, that never in my life, at school, had I a supper that I enjoyed half so much. It was a curious sight to see us all in a circle round those three poles, which were black and shining as ebony. The mother fed us all. She gave sufficient at the very outset for all our appetites, and the nice slices of onion, potato, cabbage, and small bits of white bread, brown bread, crust and crumb, all mixed with the savoury limbs of the old hen, made us a capital meal.

I have seen many public dinners since then, at which mayors and corporations have smacked their lips, and partaken of turtle soup, venison, and game; aye, and I have seen many an active dance afterwards in the ballrooms of state and fashion, but never was I at one of them without thinking of my first supper with the gipsies in the green Hundred Lane, and the merry game we afterwards had.

The first thing was a race between Jin, the youngest girl, and myself, to the end of the lane and back. Jin beat me hollow. I could not run with her, though she and I were of a similar age. She was like an antelope; and from the very start she discovered she had the race all to herself; and, looking back, she laughed at all my efforts; and in the stead of a race, it was, "Catch me, boy, catch me, if you can!" That was not easily done. The next thing was jumping over an osier bar. I thought I should stand a good chance; but here again I was made to feel my own deficiency.

Then I saw the boys have a game of wrestling; and then, to end our evening amusement, we had the great tall gipsy bring out a cremona violin, and set us all to dancing. Here I beat them, for I could dance indeed. My ears were in my feet, and I did not mind showing them what I could do, so that, before we had done our wild gallop, they were all lost in admiration at my solo.

Such was my first wild evening among the gipsies. Let men say what they will, or think as they will, Jack, Jim, and Barnaby were now my brothers and companions, and Mog and Jin my sisters; and though I had been brought up in the school of Mr. Edmund Rogers, my first holiday of life was truly spent at the gipsies' encampment.

My gipsy-bed was without a bedstead. It was without much making. It was straw, and nothing else. And what else in the summer did a lad require? Jack and Jim lay on one heap, Barnaby and I on the other. The reader may think this a curious fact, but it will serve to show how yet the grace of God was with me, for though I was in a gipsy's tent and with gipsy lads, before I lay me down to sleep, I repeated aloud, as I had been taught by my mother, the Evening Hymn.

My sleep was sound, though for a long time I thought of the anxiety my parents would feel at the uncertainty of my lot. The very excitement of the day had been enough to make me uneasy; so that straw was a sufficient bed for such a young vagrant as myself.

But I had a pleasant dream. It was a dream of freedom, and I had then an idea that I should one day be king of the gipsies. I remember seeing myself seated on a magnificent throne, surrounded by armies of warriors clad in armour, and yet, whilst on that throne, I was somehow peeling willow sticks, and Mog was my queen. My dream was interrupted, as I thought, by the neighing of a war charger, and I heard a voice calling me to horse, to mount and lead the way; in which state I awoke, and heard an ass braying in the lane, and the master gipsy's voice calling upon us to arise and prepare for a journey before breakfast. So the dream was changed for bustling activity, and it was not, "We gipsies lead a life of ease," but simply, "Gipsies journey where they please."

We did not take long to wash or dress, or pack up and be off. It was all done in half an hour - tents taken down - bundles bound up - the donkeys harnessed - the ropes for traces, an old truck for a cart, and like a primitive

patriarch of the East, see Mr. Gibson and his wife, Jack, Jim, and Barnaby, and Mog, Jin, and myself, all hastening out of the lane. The broken boiler in the centre of the tent was taken up and swung beneath the cart.

Journeying by lane, track and byway

How many men divested of their fine clothes would be better than Jonas Gibson? We were like snails - we carried our concealment on our backs. We journeyed before breakfast from the Hundred Lane to Norton Wood, and encamped again just as the gamekeeper was coming into the lane against the thicket.

"Morning, master Gibson! What have you got for breakfast?"

"Just what you see hanging out of the pot, cabbages and turnips, a little salt, hot water, and some nettle tea, and if you wish to have a cup you are welcome."

"Not I, master Gibson, I have been on the lookout for a young gentleman, who they say has got off from school into the woods and cannot be found. But they do add that he ran away by reason of the unkind treatment, and being rather of a melancholy character he is not unlikely to hang himself."

"Poor fellow, I hope he will do no such thing. But boys are not such despairing fools as men. There is in a boy's heart a buoyancy of hope, and a dependence upon others, which never leaves them whilst they are boys."

"Ah! Master Gibson, and I am dependent upon you for the very place I am in. You first taught me to shoot; you first taught me how to catch a hare, and how to catch a poacher; and yet you always used to say to me, 'Tom, fidelity alone can make a good servant.'"

" I never taught you how to be a poacher, Tom! I only taught you how poachers caught a hare, how they set their snares, and how you might take the poachers themselves."

"That's true, master Gibson."

"Tom, have you got a rabbit in your pocket?"

"I have two, master Gibson. The foxes spare too many of them to my mind. You are welcome to them. How is Mog?"

Mog had hid herself in the tent as soon as the game-keeper came up. Why or wherefore, let those who are learned in female witcheries declare. But this I know, that young as I was, I had a precocity of mind as inquiring as any simple man could imagine. Why did Mog bolt into the tent the moment she saw the gamekeeper?

I was not too young just to fancy that Mog absconded because she wished to be missed, nor yet that Tom, the gamekeeper, had a liking for Mog; and somehow I felt also that if I were in Tom's situation, and a fine fellow, with a green jacket and velveteens, with a gun under my arm, and permission to shoot rabbits to make the pot boil, that I might feel an aspiring hope that Mog would make a very good wife, though she was a gipsy's daughter.

"Do you want Mog to skin the rabbits?"

The young man blushed, and looked a little flushed, and actually said to the gipsy, to my utter astonishment, "I beg your pardon, No! no! I did not mean that. No. I can skin the rabbits. Only I missed your daughter."

In the lee of Norton Wood

"Mog," said the gipsy, as Tom handed the rabbits to him, and seeming to recover himself from some unpleasant feeling, "here, take these rabbits to your mother, tell her to prepare them for our evening meal."

Mog bolted with the rabbits, and carried them directly to her mother. Tom looked at her as though he would have spoken, but the gipsy's eye was upon him, and he dared not.

It was evident that Gibson had some command over the gamekeeper, of a very superior character, although he was a fine stout young fellow, and looked as though he need not be afraid.

He turned round, and took the gamekeeper's arm. I shall never forget it, for I have known what it is to have a duke, a lord, a great man, put his arm in my own, and take me away with him, as if he meant to be familiar or respectful, when he was all the while only desirous to escape some unpleasant observation. I say that, even then, Gibson, the gipsy, looked as proud as a duke when he took the arm of the gamekeeper, and walked with him into the wood.

Oh, curiosity, curiosity! I almost wished myself a hare, to bop under the ferns and run along the thicket, just that I might hide myself in the bush, to hear what those two were talking about; but I was afraid of being taken for what I was, a bit of a sly fox, and so being shot for my curiosity.

Luckily for me, as I was looking all amazement after them, a pat on the back made me jump; and Mog, with a merry voice, said, "Come, brother, come, don't stand staring into the wood, come and learn to make a breakfast and a basket." And she popped into her brother's tent, and I after her, where we found a good substantial breakfast of bread and hot milk already prepared for us.

In the heart of Norton Wood

We sat down and ate our breakfast with great gusto; and though I confess my mind was all thought about Mog, and Tom, and Gibson, and the gamekeeper; and hares and rabbits; and lords and ladies, and I know not what; yet I dared not say what I thought, because Mog herself appeared to have forgotten all about it; chatted away about the work to be done, where we were to go, who would sell the most baskets, or make them best; but, strange to say, she ate no breakfast herself.

Mog went out of the tent for something, and I heard her sobbing in her mother's tent, and the old woman seemed to sooth her.

Presently Mog came back again, her dark eye was very red within the lashes, and we all maintained a perfect silence and a gentleness towards her. As soon as we had finished breakfast, she set us all to work.

"Come, I must take you in hand, Master Harry, and teach you how to make a basket." She showed me how to lay the bottom thereof, and to carry up the uprights, how exactly to bend them, and especially the larger and stouter ones, and then how to plait them in and out, in and out. Two or three times she said to me, "You seem very stupid this morning, Harry, you seem stupid." And all the while I was thinking of her and the gamekeeper, but I dared not say so. So I took it as a boy does a rap on the head, for inattention, and to work I went.

Nothing is done without labour - nothing at all - and I thought that I ought to try and earn something to pay for my breakfast. That thought put me into the right train, and soon she began to say: "Come, that will do. There, you understand. That's right. Work on, and mother will be pleased again."

And the mother did come; but just as she came in, we heard the gamekeeper's gun, and she turned away from our work and listened. We all listened. I know not what made us listen, but I suppose mother's being so intent made us so too.   In another minute, the gipsy's voice was heard.

"Boys! - Tom, Jim, and Barnaby - boys! Come here! Come here!"

Away went the boys.   I was going too, but Mog caught hold of me, saying, "Harry, stay with me."   It was magic. It was impossible for me to run away, for Mog looked very pale, trembled, then sat down, listened, and sighed.   She tried to work, but at last said, "Harry, I fear there is something amiss.   But stay with me; there are plenty gone into the wood."

Whatever one may feel about the accuracy of this story, even today, two hundred years later, many of the places he writes about seem to have changed very little.

By the lane leading to Norton Wood

The mother's instinct had caught alarm from her husband and she had gone into her tent.

The most unbelievable part of this encounter relates to the language being spoken. Gipsies at this time spoke a distinct tongue called Romani. Though they may very well have been bi-lingual, especially the gipsy father, surely their language amongst themselves would have been predominantly their own. Yet Steggall mentions little of this. Maybe he is just trying to simplify matters for the reader, but all we are offered by way of a different vocabulary are words like the old English 'younker', meaning youngster.

Chapter 3 ~ The accident

How very soon is a house of joy turned into a house of mourning! Mog and I sat listening with beating hearts for what was coming. I thinking more of her than she of me, for if the truth could be told, my presence was only on purpose that she might not be alone. Mog would every minute put her head down as if to pick up a willow-stick, and I could perceive it was only to listen to the sound, if any could be caught, of coming footsteps.

Jin was the first to hear them, for she was outside, standing against the gate leading into the wood, and she came rushing, or rather bolting, into the tent: "They are coming! They are coming! I can hear father's voice, saying: 'take care, Tom. Gently with his legs, Barnaby. Jim, take care of the gun.'"

Poor Mog! Poor Mog! Her face was as wild as that of a terrified lamb, which, being outside the fold, sees the wolf coming, and cannot get to its dam. I, no longer liking to stay where I was, passed Mog very quietly, and she took no notice of me, for I crept round the other side of the canvas, and walked directly up to the gate. I heard them coming. I first saw that which I did not wish Mog to see; so I turned round, and with my hand beckoned to her to go back into the tent. But this only made her so much the more intent.

I would have drawn a curtain between them if I could, for I saw Gibson and his two boys bearing the body of the game-keeper, whose head and face seemed covered with blood.

Gibson said, "Up with you boy, and run and tell mother we are here." There wanted not that to tell her, for one of the wildest shrieks that ever rung in Norton Wood thrilled through all our hearts as poor Mog caught sight of the bleeding head, and vented her whole strength of body and spirit in that cry. It was not a wail - It was not a howl - It was not a cry for help. It was a piercing shriek such as a being gives who sees a gulf and knows nothing can save him from it. Poor Mog! Poor Mog! That shriek was but one effort, one utterance, and she herself was on the earth insensible.

I believe that the gipsy himself would have dropped the body had not that very shriek had an effect upon the seemingly dead, which he had no idea of. Those eyes opened, the head moved, and a struggling shudder ran through the frame of the youth, which was even more overpowering to the gipsy than the voice of despair which came from the daughter.

"He is alive, boys! He is alive. He heard Mog's cry. Come, bear him along; bear him along. There, that will do, that will do."

Nothing could be more gentle than the gipsies' bearing, nothing more touching and tender than the whole scene, which, though I now describe it when I am grown old and grey, and have passed through such scenes of joy and sorrow as after pages must describe, is yet as vivid before me as if it were but a scene of yesterday, a transaction of the very day in which I live.

Into that tent on a bed already prepared was the body of the young gamekeeper borne, laid thereupon, and now came such a scene as convinced me gipsies have hearts as well as we have, at least Gibson had. A tear was on the hard-featured man's cheek as he looked at the ghastly countenance. He felt the pulse; he found it beating.

"Tom, run you down to Ixworth with all speed to Mr. Rowe, the surgeon: simply say to him that Squire Norton's game-keeper has happened with an accident, a gun-shot wound, and is in the gipsies' tent at the east end of Norton Wood. Speed, boy, speed."

"Jim, go you to old Mrs Sealey's, near The Dog, and tell her that her son is ill, and wants to see her at the gipsies' tent."

"And you, Barnaby... Yes." And the gipsy paused, and placed his hand upon his head as if it ached. "Yes, Barnaby, yes. Go you to the Rectory. I know not who is the minister, but I know poor Sealey was always at his church on Sunday, and a good fellow too; and tell him there is a dying man at the gipsies' tent."

Sealey probably lived in the keeper's cottage, which lay to the west of the wood, close by Crawley Hall Farm. A track ran down to the wood from the cottage, which is named on early maps. There was another area of woodland to the west of this cottage named Crawley Grove, but this was felled some time between 1840 and 1880.

Sealey's mother is reputed to have lived in Heath Road, which begins opposite **The Dog** public house.

The parson referred to, and named later in the chapter was the Reverend William Clerke M.A., who was appointed to the Rectory of Norton in April 1797. Norton had been remarkably unfortunate in their appointment of a parson. Following the death of Reverend William Oldham in 1795, the Rev. Wm. Kendall only lived one more year and his successor, Thomas Veasey, resigned after only a few weeks.

If, as seems likely, Steggall was born in 1791, then the events of this chapter would most probably have occurred in the summer of 1799.

The doctor named in this chapter both as Mr. Rowe and Mr. Rose, may be one of the details Steggall had not remembered correctly. The nearest surgeons by either name we were able to trace worked at Hartest, Eye and Sudbury. In fact, it would not have been necessary to send all the way to Ixworth for a doctor, as a surgeon by the name of Clayton was reported as marrying and living in Norton in 1796 (Bury Post).

And then the gipsy sighed or groaned, but I diverted his thoughts, for seeing he had given them all something to do, I quietly said, "And what am I to do, Mr. Gibson?"

"Well, young lad," he said, "I wish you were somewhere else than where you are, for I know not what to do with you. You had better go a begging."

"For what, sir?"

"For some linen rags."

"Take my shirt out of the boiler."

"That won't do."

"Why not?"

"It would be found out."

"Why so?"

"Because the very rags would prove it to be better linen than gipsies wear."

"Well, what then?"

"You would bring me into trouble. Boy, don't you know yet, that nobody believes a gipsy."

"I do."

"Yes, you believe me, and trust me, but children are mostly afraid of me. You are not."

"No, you have been kind to me."

"It will not always do to trust the kindness of a gipsy; but go, you must go and ask somewhere for some linen. Go up to Norton Hall, boy, take the lane down to the left, cross along the foot of the valley, and you will come up into the drift way leading to the Hall, you may be of some service: off with you."

This was the first begging expedition I ever went upon in my life, and as it was for another, and that for the life of another, I felt no compunction at the job I had to undertake. Yet somehow I was an awkward beggar. I felt I was, and my heart was filled with something like fear. Yet off I went, only just taking a peep at poor Mog before I started. She was reviving. Her dark mother, with her

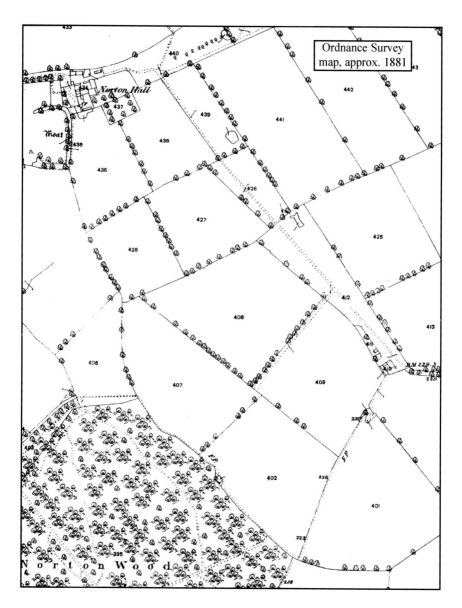

Ordnance Survey
map, approx. 1881

swarthy hands, was smoothing down her hair, and actually, with all a mother's tenderness, saying, "Come Mog, come! Cheer up! Cheer up! Hope! Hope! Don't cast it all away! He is not dead! He is not dead! Father would not have sent for a surgeon if he were dead!

Tom is gone for the doctor; Jim is gone for his mother; Barnaby is gone somewhere!"

"Where, mother, where?"

"I think for the minister of the parish, the Rev. Clarke."

"Ah! Mother, is it so? Then he will die."

"No, Mog, not the more for that. Rectors don't kill people."

"No, but they bury them."

"Poor Mog! They would have them live."

"Yes, mother, yes! I should like him to live; yes, to live a little longer here; I don't wish him to die. Do you think that he will die?"

"I hope not. Harry, where are you going?"

"I am going a-begging, mother."

"We do not want anything, mother. Why should dear little Harry go a-begging?"

"Don't be sorry, dear Mog, I am only going to the Hall to ask for some linen rags. You ought to be glad."

"But will he die, Harry, will he die?"

"Oh no," said I, "Certainly not!" And I spake with a kind of confidence that was more cheering than any kindness of the mother.

She looked hard at me; she thought she saw a gleam of hope; she put forth her dark but yet livid hand; and, though she did not say, come here, she drew me to her and kissed me for my comfort. It did me good, and it did her good likewise. It relieved her aching heart; it made me rejoice that I could give her comfort and I said, "There, Mog, you are better now. Do not delay me, or perhaps the surgeon will be here before I am back."

She let me go, and off I went. The birds were singing around me, the skylarks rose high in the air, the little warbler sent forth the joyful praise of his heart. I was sent forth upon a hopeful expedition, and, though but eight years old, to myself I was much older, and I seemed to be gifted with a strength I never had before.

Down along the lane I ran, sprang over the stile, laying my hands upon the upper bar, took the footpath along the ploughed field, then a summer-till, then across another field of pasture, and over into the drift-way with a leap, that at once got me such a cut across the back for my agility, that it made me blubber most tremendously.

"You good for nothing young dog!" said a gentleman, who was driving a lady in a hooded chaise, just going up the hill, "you nearly had thrown my horse down upon his knees. What are you doing here, you young vagabond? I'll teach you to frighten folks, I will!" And he gave me another thwack which made me leap over the stile again, but not run back. No; I had an errand, I had a task, a duty to perform, and no thwacks, although they made me smart and blubber, could make me forget the duty I had to perform. So I stood still, but out of reach of the whip.

"What are you doing here, you young scoundrel?"

"I am going up to the Hall."

"Are you? Let me catch you there, that's all!"

A quick thought struck me that it might be the squire and his lady, who had gone down to the farm, and were going to the town of Ixworth, so forgetting my smart, I said, "I was going to ask for a few rags for the game-keeper, who has happened with an accident."

"What gamekeeper, boy?"

"Your own, sir. He was in Norton Wood this morning, searching for a young gentleman who is missing, and has happened with an accident."

"Is it Sealey?"

"I think it is, sir."

"Did the gun burst?"

"I don't know, sir; but father found him and took him to his tent, sir, and has sent for Mr. Rose, the surgeon. He is very bad."

"What did your father do in Norton Wood?"

"He walked into the wood with Sealey, sir."

"Oh, you are sure of that, are you?"

"Yes, sir, I saw them go in together."

"It might be that he went in search of that young lad of whom I heard yesterday. Well, well! Come, boy, come; I'll forgive you. Go up to the Hall."

"Don't cry, poor boy," said the lady, "I'll give you some rags."

So, I forgave the squire for his injustice towards me, for the sake of poor Sealey, and Mog, and Gibson, and Tom, and Jim, and Barnaby.

The squire, described in the book both as *'Squire Norton'* and *'Squire N_____,'* would probably have been a William Nunn who advertised a sale of stock at Norton Hall in the Bury Post in 1803. Earlier references show him to have been a parish constable; not a magistrate as Steggall describes. This seems a reasonable mistake for him to have made, in attempting to remember events from his childhood over 50 years earlier.

There are many inconsistencies in the book regarding the names of people. Notice how the eldest gipsy boy's name has changed from *Jack* to *Tom.*

I followed the yellow-bodied and hooded one-horse chaise up to the hall. I had even the politeness to run and open the gate for the squire, though he had given me such a thwack as made a great leviathan weal across my back; yet I had in view the rags which he promised me. I thought of the gipsy's orders, and the poor gamekeeper's condition.

The lady also dropped me a penny as she passed through the gate, and I thought she looked as if she would have healed the wounds her rough - not to say cruel - husband had inflicted.

Norton Hall today

I bore the smart for the sake of the charitable rags, which were to comfort the sick, and I even condemned myself when I picked up the penny - not for the thought of a bribe, but because I did not look before I leaped. I have leapt over many stiles since - have gone through all kinds of dangers - but never leapt into a lane without thinking of who might be on the other side of the gate or hedge.

"Boy, stay there at the gate, I will come and speak to you. John, take my horse."

The squire drove into the yard, his mistress got out, and he came back and spake to me.

"What's your name, younker?"

That was a question I had never had put to me before. But I had taken the gipsy's habit, I had given up my own kin, I had fled from the name and nature of a schoolboy, and had become one of Master Gibson's family.

"My name is Henry Gibson."

"What parish do you belong to?"

"All parishes!"

"Where is your father?"

"On the other side of your honour's wood."

"Is Sealey very bad?"

"I should think so. He is shot in the back of the neck. Father has sent for the surgeon, and for Sealey's mother, and, I think, for the Rev. Clarke, the clergyman."

"For the clergyman? A gipsy send for a clergyman! Are you sure he has done so? The man's a better man than I thought him. But I fear poor Sealey must be very bad indeed."

"Father is a very kind father, sir, and I think your gamekeeper Sealey is more indebted to him than you are aware of, sir. He was once a boy under Mr. Gibson's tuition."

Just then came the lady bringing the rags; and, to be sure, my young heart could have made me jump up and kiss her; for she brought me some nice fruit, and told me to come again tomorrow for some more. I say I could have kissed her, and yet I dare not, for my old sheepskin and tarpaulin trousers; but I cried.

"Why do you cry?"

"Because you are so very kind."

"Go - go!" said the squire. "My dear, you are too tender by half. You know not what vagabonds these gipsies are. This very boy may be a good-for-nothing thief!"

"I do not believe he would cry if he were so bad."

"I am not bad," said I.

"Go about your business, boy, and tell your father I shall walk across and inquire into the case. I shall not be long before I come; so be off with you."

I made a very polite dancing master's bow to the lady; and though I did not like the squire so well as I did her ladyship, yet I did my best, and had he kicked me, I had got the rags, and my heart was happy.

Away I went; nor did I stop my trotting until I arrived at the Green Lane again. I ran into Mog's tent. She was sitting with her face in her hands, and rocking herself to and fro, as if deep grief was in her heart. I saw it was so.

"Mog, here are the rags. And look, I see the doctor coming up the lane; and there is an old woman too, walking along the path with some gentleman."

The hopes of Mog were with the doctor.

"Boy! Come and hold my horse!"

"Yes, sir." And I had now the pleasure of being useful.

The doctor's horse, however, was a little too frisky for a boy of eight years old to walk about with; he seemed, too, as if he was disposed to try my courage, for he stamped with his foot, and pawed the ground and pranced about, and feeling my hand tremble, he reared, and fairly lifted me off my legs; but I did not let go, but called out, and Gibson soon came out of the tent and took the bridle in his hand, and told me to go to the doctor.

I ran into the tent to take my first lesson in surgery: and, being a very tender-hearted boy, I felt too much, for when the surgeon asked me to hold Sealey's head up, and I saw the wound I confess I turned so sick I was forced to run quickly out of the tent to the ditch; and no shame either - I was sick.

Mother gave me a little brandy, and at the same time told me to go in again directly. I obeyed, and the brandy calming my stomach, I was now anxious to render assistance.

The wound was washed, bits of the wadding extracted, and the poor mother, who stood outside the tent, and handed the water to me, and I to the doctor, was very anxious to know what the doctor thought.

Doctors don't say much. Their business is to do what they can in the case, and as quickly as they can. Neither did the doctor ask many questions; he simply said, "I cannot think how the man could inflict this wound himself."

All this time poor young Sealey was insensible, and though he evidently breathed, yet he was unable to speak. Gibson was leading the doctor's horse, and when the clergyman came up to the tent and asked the doctor how the poor man was, and learnt that he was insensible, he only asked us if we could any of us read. I told him I could; and he gave me a little book on "Visitation of the Sick," and then walked to the other tent. There he found Mog and her mother. He went into the tent and very kindly conversed with them.

He was one of those good men who taught that all things should be taken with submission to God's will, and he said to poor Mog, "I do hope that it is God's will the young man should recover; and I will pray, with you, that if it be not His will, we may all be resigned, and that we may depend upon Him for the best."

He was a good young clergyman and the sequel will show that he was a wise one as well, for poor Mog's faith was put to the test in a very few hours after this transaction; and she had nothing which ever did console her so much as the good advice and kind attention of the clergyman and his family.

The squire's voice was heard in the lane, and, soon after he came, affairs took such a turn that we were all confounded.

The village of Norton was no stranger to suffering. A decade earlier, a fire had destroyed a number of houses, making a fifth of the population homeless. An entry in the baptism register states: *1788. On the 3rd of April in this year a great fire happened in Norton, about 10 o'clock in the forenoon, and continued burning several days. Nearly 40 buildings of various kinds were consumed. No lives were lost. It broke out in the house of John Chapman, shopkeeper in Norton Street.*

The Ipswich Journal reported briefly on the 5th explaining that the fire had started at the baking office. A more detailed report the following week described how the blower had been left on, and Mr. Chapman's bakery destroyed, along with the farms of Mr. Booty and Mr. Burt, and the houses and outhouses of Mr. Ship and Mr. Grimwood. *"By the above melancholy catastrophe 20 poor families are deprived of their habitations and reduced to the greatest distress, most of their furniture being destroyed. Not one of the houses were insured except that where the accident begun."*

A subscription was begun for the benefit of the sufferers, led by Ald. Patteson of Norwich who was Lord of the Manor at the time. The West Suffolk Record office has correspondence relating to this appeal.

The Keeper's cottage at Crawley Hall Farm once stood here, at the top of the line of trees to the right which runs down to Norton Wood

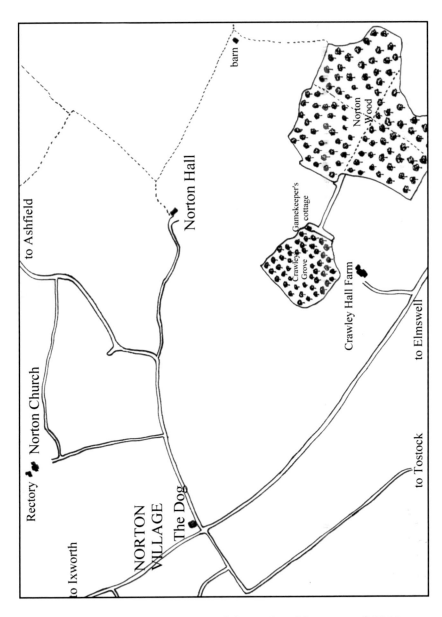

A map of Norton constructed from the tithe map of 1841

52

Chapter 4 ~ The Squire

The arrival of the squire created a general stir in the gipsy camp, for the squire was a great man, a magistrate, a good man, so reckoned, though as squires sometimes do, and masters and mistresses likewise, he took the law into his own hands, and administered the lash where he had no business so to do.

The squire's, "Humph, Gibson!" created a pause in the curate's sermon to poor Mog. That voice of autocratic sound, called all attention. It was a call for us all to come forth, and out we all went, save the doctor, who, I dare say, said within himself, as doctors frequently do, "I have got a case to attend to more important than the squire's command, at all events let the squire come to me, or send for me, or ask for me, and I shall then be of some importance." So he remained in the gipsy's tent.

Gibson also was holding the surgeon's horse, and he came very leisurely with the prancing little steed up towards the squire.

"Gibson! Come here!"

"Yes, your honour! But I cannot leave the horse."

"Then bring him with you."

Now the squire might have gone to Gibson, but just imagine three tents pitched in a green lane, and the squire standing between two of them, and calling Gibson to come to him. Gibson had no alternative but to lead the fiery little pony up to the tents. He did not like the look of our habitations; he snorted and would have reared, but the gipsy's strong right arm kept his head so down that the pony could not lift his fore legs. No sooner, however, had he brought his head to the squire's presence, than without more ado he lifted up his hind legs and sent them smack into Mog's tent, and a pair of holes held the little fellow's legs in an instant so that he could not extricate them.   Then there was a kicking, a plunging, a snapping, and cracking of the hoops, an overturning of the tent, and such a scramble that the squire jumped into the ditch, and came out again with something like a pair of highlows of mud over his beautiful velveteen buskins.

The little animal was extricated as well as could be, but he never after could be persuaded to approach a gipsy's tent.

The squire was not a little angry.   "Boy, bring some clean straw."   I had to rub the mud off his worship's feet.

"There, that will do."

The surgeon, hearing a hubbub, had come out of the sick man's tent, for had the pony put his hind legs into that instead of into Mog's tent, it would have been a very awkward thing.

"I hope that you are not hurt, Mr. N____."

Using the abbreviation 'Mr. N____' may be an attempt to conceal the identity of the squire. Alternatively, it may be just that he has forgotten the name.   More likely, it is a typical affectation employed in books at this time to give a pretence of anomynolising the name, which must have been familiar to his local readers, at least.

"Fortunately I am not, but why do you keep such a vicious brute of a pony as that?   He is very dangerous."

"I do not think that he has any vice.   I never knew him vicious; he is very high-spirited, but very quiet.   I am sorry he has occasioned you such dirty feet."

"Yes, I suppose so," said the squire, "and had my shins been broken..."

"Undoubtedly I should have done my best to set them right."

"Well, well, it is very unpleasant, for I was going to the

magistrates' sitting at Ixworth, and now I must go home again first.   But how is your patient?"

Mog drew very near to the squire and looked very anxiously at the doctor.

"My patient is very bad - and if he remain here he will die.   He is insensible, and will be so for some hours, and I think he should be removed directly."

"Do you know anything about the occasion of the accident?"

"I only know, that if it be an accident it is one of the strangest I ever heard of.   The man is shot in the back of the neck, and the cervical vertebrae are as bare in one place as if they had been scraped with a knife.   The muscles are perforated but not destroyed.   I never saw a thing so near death, inasmuch as it was almost a broken neck."

"How was it done?"

"That, squire, is to me a mystery; I cannot say how it was done."

"Do you believe the man did it himself?"

"I cannot conceive it possible that he could do it himself."

"Then I must ask you, when you get home, to tell the constable of Ixworth to meet me at the Pickerel immediately."

Ixworth, like a number of small towns at this time held petty sessions. Usually, these were held in coaching inns, being the largest available buildings, and offering refreshments to those involved. As time went on, the public thirst for the reporting of crime grew, and such small local courts more frequently found their way into the columns of the local papers. Unfortunately, around 1799, Ixworth petty sessions featured rarely, and it is no surprise that this case should not have been reported.

"I will do so, squire."

"Send Gibson to me."

Gibson came as soon as the surgeon was mounted, but he had most feelingly said, "How is the poor fellow?"

"It is a very awkward piece of business, Master Gibson, and I fear it will bring you into trouble; but the squire wants you."

"Gibson, I do not desire that you should criminate yourself, but the circumstances of this case are so suspicious that I should not do my duty to the public, if I did not issue my warrant for your apprehension. You may be quite innocent of any criminality, but you must satisfy the magistrates thereof, or be committed to prison, and if poor Sealey should not be able to make a deposition, the case will be very serious for you."

"Very well, your honour; I am ready to go to Ixworth, but do you not think we had better remove the man to his mother's house first?"

"Leave that to me, Gibson, I will send a bed or something easy for him to lie upon. I am very sorry for it."

"And so am I, your honour, and I hope to satisfy your worship and the magistrates that I had nothing to do with it."

"I wish you may, Gibson. Was there anybody but yourself with him at the time?"

"Nobody, your honour; I will tell you -"

"So much the worse, Gibson; don't tell me anything about it now, but if you have a mind to spare trouble, go down to the Pickerel at Ixworth, without delay."

"I will go directly, your honour."

"Boy," said the squire to me, "Here's sixpence for you, but take care how you jump into lanes for the future."

"I will, your honour."

"Let that boy go with you, Gibson."

"Why so, sir?"

"Because I wish it."

"He did not see the accident."

"Maybe not! But I think that boy will speak truth."

I saw Gibson look at me. I saw his blood a little stirred within him, for it was as much as to say that he would not speak the truth. There were some closer fears near the gipsy's heart concerning myself, which at the same time weighed upon his mind. Still he schooled himself well, and replied, "Well, your worship, I hope I shall speak the truth too; the boy shall go along with me. Harry, are you ready?"

The squire saw the tears start in Mog's eyes, and not only did they start in hers, but mother's also, and, therefore, they did in mine, as the squire and the minister walked away in conversation, such as I found afterwards was of a very serious character.

"Children," said Gibson, "attend to poor Sealey, and stop where you are until I come back. I cannot tell you how long that will be, but I hope things will turn out favourably."

"Husband, let me ask you one question before you go," said Mrs Gibson, "because I can endure anything when I know the worst. Did you cause the wound which poor Sealey has got or did you not?"

"I did not give him the wound, wife; nor did I intend or think of doing so. He and I were talking of some matters of great moment, and I think poor Sealey was a little passionate. I do not think he intended to strike me, but he had his gun in his hand, and it came so near my head, either in his argument or his vehemence, that I warded it off with my hand, and it swung round with him, his foot slipping at the moment, when he knocked the stock as he was falling against the stump, and the gun fell out of his hand, and when on the ground it went off. Anyone may see that the charge went along the ground, by the very ploughing of the earth and ferns close to where poor Sealey's head lay. I wish the squire had allowed me to show him how it happened. But I daresay he thinks me guilty. Do not you think so? Nothing was further from my mind. Nothing."

"Yet I fear you will have some difficulty in proving your case."

"It may be so, and should I be committed to prison, you and the boys must do the best you can; but I shall hope that poor Sealey will recover, and then all will be right."

"Oh, father, I hope he will," said Mog. "But why do they want Harry to go with you?"

"Harry," said Gibson to me, "did you say anything to the squire about it?"

"I only told him that you were in search of a young gentleman that was lost, or I thought that you had gone with Sealey into the wood for that purpose."

"Are you sure you said nothing else?"

"I don't remember that I did, unless it was something about Sealey's being indebted to you in early life, which I think I heard him say."

"Boy, you should be cautious, and not be so communicative; a close tongue makes a wise head. You are a quick little fellow, but silence is a great quality when you are not required to speak."

"I am sure I did not mean to do you any harm."

"That I am sure of; but you may have done yourself some, as well as me."

"Oh, never mind me! I shall take no hurt. It is you only, and Mog, and Jin, and mother here that I care about."

"And is there such a spirit in you, boy? Then come along with me, and we will share the danger together."

For the first time in my life I felt a hero - as if I was

going actually to fight a battle upon principle, and that principle, the defence of the oppressed.

So, shaking hands with poor tearful Mog and mother, and telling Jin to take care of Tom Sealey, and give my love to Tom, and Jim and Barnaby, off we started for Ixworth.

The long town of Ixworth was crowded with folks coming to the sessions, and the report had reached the town that a murder had been committed in Norton Wood, and it was said that Gibson, the gipsy, was the perpetrator. Some said that it was the poor lad who had escaped from school who was murdered, and this very report had gone, like wildfire, to Wyverstone. Some said it was a female, but the most part said there had been a quarrel between Gibson and one of Squire Norton's gamekeepers, and that the gipsy had seized the man's gun and shot him through the head; so that when Gibson and I

walked into the street, we were hooted, and pelted, and so roughly handled, that had not the constables and some few gentlemen fought stoutly for us, I verily believe we should neither of us have reached the Pickerel alive. As it was, the mob were so vociferous that the magistrates, and Squire Cartwright of the Abbey, had to address them, and correct them, and assure them there was nothing but a case of suspicion before them, and that it was very un-English to condemn anyone without a fair trial.

We found protection in the presence of the gentlemen in the court. The very first person called as a witness was myself.

"Boy, what age are you?" said the chairman.

"Just eight, sir."

And at that moment I caught sight of the constable of Walsham, who had seen poor me acting the idiot deaf and dumb boy the day before. I felt that now I was in a mess, as the constable said in my hearing, "Oh, what a young rascal that is! It was but yesterday he was deaf and dumb. I think their worships ought to know that." But he did not interrupt the proceedings.

Barns at the rear of The Pickerel

"Do you understand the nature of an oath, boy?"

"No, I don't."

"Then simply take this affirmation."

The constable looked at me, as if to say - 'I wish it may be worth having, but I doubt it.'

"Did you not come to my house for some rags this morning?"

"I did, squire."

"Did you not tell me that you saw the gamekeeper and the gipsy in conversation before they went into the wood?"

"Yes sir."

" How long have you known Sealey, the gamekeeper?"

"Never saw him before this morning."

"How, then, did you know that the gamekeeper had been in debt to your father?"

"I did not know it."

"You are a young liar, I fear, and are afraid to speak the truth!"

"No, I a'nt."

"Then tell me the truth.   Do you mean to say that you did not say my gamekeeper was in debt to your father?"

"I might say that father had obliged him."

"Come, younker - obliged him?   Are you sure you did not say in debt, or indebted to him?"

"I might say some such thing - but what of that?"

"What of that, boy; do you ask me a question?"

"Yes; if you please, sir; why not?"

I was quite unacquainted with courts of justice, and I never felt as a prisoner, though I did feel very queer before the constable of Walsham, whom I had deceived. I was reprimanded for impertinence, and I had no idea or intention thereof, for I thought mine but a fair question.

But there must be an order in everything, so I had no right to question the squire, though he might ask me anything; but I could not help saying, "Pray, sir, why did you give me a sixpence this morning, if you think me such a bad boy?"

The squire blushed, for the court might think I had been bribed to make my appearance and bear witness against my own father, and that the squire had given me money for such a purpose. There was evidently a little embarrassment in the squire's manner.

"What was the nature of the debt, boy, which you spoke of - how much?   In what sum?"

"In no sum at all."

"What! No sum of money?"

"No sir."

"What then?   What did you hear the gamekeeper say?"

"Something like this: 'You first taught me how to shoot - you first taught me how to set a snare - and you first taught me how to catch a poacher.'"

There was evidently some stir in the court and I heard the constable of Walsham say, "A young dog - he's no fool either!"

"And this is all you meant when you said that Tom Sealey was indebted to your father?"

The magistrates conversed awhile, and a paper was handed to the squire. It was evidently a betrayal of me to the magistrates in having pretended to be a deaf and dumb boy.

"Let the constable of Walsham be sworn."

"Do you know the last witness?"

"I do."

"Will you swear to him?"

"I will; anywhere."

"When did you see him last?"

"Yesterday morning."

"Where?"

"In the Hundred Lane, in Wyverstone."

"What did you do there?"

"I went in search of a young gentleman who had run away from school, and it was supposed had got into the woods."

"Did you see the witness at the gipsy's tent?"

"I did."

"In what condition was he?"

"In the condition of a deaf and dumb boy."

"How do you know he was deaf and dumb?"

"I know now, your honour, that he was not so, and that he must be a most artful, wicked, young dog, for he deceived the constable of Badwell as well as myself and looked exactly like an idiot. He could not speak, he could not hear, and laughed just like a fool; and pulled the peel off an osier twig exactly like an insane person."

"Do you hear this, my lad?"

"Yes, your honour; I do."

"And pray what was it for?"

"Only for a bit of fun sir."

"And are you in the habit of using such deceptions?"

"No, sir; I never did so before."

"What did you do it for?"

"For what I got given to me."

"What was that?"

"A penny, sir."

"So you obtained money under false pretences, did you?"

"I did not beg; I did not take any money. The constable gave the penny to my poor sister."

"Is that true?"

"Yes, your honour."

There was here a roar of laughter in the court against the constable, and at my expense, for they all looked at me, and at my marvellous powers of deception. I only know that I felt a little ashamed, and heartily wished myself out of court, but my trial was not yet over, though for the present the constable of Ixworth was ordered to take charge of me.

As there was no other witness against Gibson, the magistrates were a little puzzled, for it was evident that the obtuse though well-meaning squire had mistaken the meaning of my words, and he wanted to elicit a motive for the murderous attack which seemingly had been made upon the gamekeeper; but evidently failing in this, they did not exactly know what to say about the case; but the clergyman was there, and the doctor. So the latter was first called and sworn.

"You are a medical man?"

"Yes."

"You live at Ixworth?"

"I do."

"How did you know that the gamekeeper was shot?"

"I was sent for."

"By whom?"

"The prisoner Gibson.   He told me simply that the gamekeeper had shot himself accidentally; and that their tent was behind your honour's wood."

"You have seen the patient?"

"I have."

"Is it your opinion that the man shot himself?"

"It is my opinion that he did not; that he could not, under ordinary circumstances, have done so."

"Where is the wound?"

"Directly in the back of the neck."

"Let the lad be called."

I was then placed before the magistrates.

"Boy, did you see the gipsy and the gamekeeper go into the wood together?"

"I did."

"What did they go for?"

"That I don't know."

"Were they angry with one another?"

"I should think not."

"Why?"

"Because I saw the gamekeeper give father two rabbits."

"Are you sure of that?   Did you see anything paid for the rabbits?"

"Nothing."

"Do you know if they were sold to him?"

"They were not sold, but given to him."

"For nothing?"

"For nothing that I know of."

"Who took the rabbits?"

"Sister Mog."

"What for?"

"To skin them, and tell mother to get them ready for our suppers."

"Now, boy, do you say that your father and the game-keeper had no high words?"

"I did not hear any."

"Did they look angry one with another?"

"Not that I know of."

"Did you hear the report of the gun?"

"Yes."

"How long after that was it that you knew the game-keeper was shot?"

"A few minutes.   I heard father's voice calling to his sons to come to him into the wood.   They went."

"Did you go with them?"

"No."

"How long was it before they came back?"

"Ten minutes."

"What did your father then do?"

"Sent for the surgeon; sent off for his mother; sent off for the clergyman; and sent me for rags to your hall."

There was evidently a stir here in the court, and the gipsy was by some looked upon, as he deserved to be, as a most humane man. The surgeon was then recalled.

"Do you consider that the case is dangerous?"

"Decidedly so."

"Is the man insensible?"

"He is."

"Will he recover his senses?"

"I cannot say; but I think he will."

"Can you tell us how long it may probably be?"

"I cannot possibly say; I expect that fever will ensue; and in all probability the man will be delirious for some time.   If we can subdue the fever, I expect there will be, even if he should sink under the blow, some interval of a luminous character, preceding either his death or his recovery."

The magistrates then conferred together, and at last they said, by their chairman -

"Gibson, it is evident you were in company with this poor man when he was shot, and you have heard the evidence of the lad and the surgeon. We give you full credit for humanity in the case after the blow - but we are decidedly dissatisfied, as yet as to the cause of that blow. Strong suspicion is attached to the case. You are not bound to say anything, but you may now ask the lad or the surgeon any questions you please."

Gibson looked at me and said, "The boy has spoken the truth: I have no questions to put to him. But I must ask the surgeon a question on his oath."

"Do you mean to say, Mr. Rose, and do you mean to swear, that it was impossible that such a wound could be accidentally given?"

"I do not mean to swear that you might not have accidentally shot the man, but I mean to say that I do not believe that he accidentally shot himself."

"Do you mean to swear that it was impossible?"

"No, I only swear that I believe, according to the situation of the wound, that no man could have done it himself."

"Gibson, you are at liberty to make any disclosures you please, but we do not desire you should criminate yourself. You may say anything you like, but whatever you do say will be used in court for or against you, as it may appear in evidence."

"I should be sorry, gentlemen, to have it go forth that I am a murderer. I have known Sealey from a boy and his father before him, and I never knew a nicer boy - nor do I think your honour has a better gamekeeper in your service.   What the lad says is true, I taught him how snares were set because I had often found them, but I never set any in my life.   I taught him how to rear pheasants, because I had reared them myself; and I taught him how to watch for a poacher, not because I had been a poacher, but because I had seen them taken.   I liked the boy, and I am sure he is a faithful servant.   Your honour gives him leave to keep the rabbits down, and now and then he gives me one.   This morning he gave me two, and he said to me, 'Master Gibson, I want to speak to you.'   He had told me about the young gentleman who was lost, but we did not go into the wood on that account. He wanted to speak to me more particularly.   Yes, gentlemen, when we got some way into the wood, he turned round to me, and said, 'Gibson, I love your daughter, and if you will let her stay with my mother, I will marry her.'

Now, I did not wish my daughter to marry him, though I believe she loves him too - why, I do not choose to say, and I dare say you will excuse it.

The young man was hurt - he was a little put out, as was natural, and he flourished his gun in the air.   It came a little too near my head, I warded it off, and just at that time the young man's foot slipt into the rut of the bushway in the wood, and he fell.   When he fell, he knocked the stock against a tree, and I suppose that the cock caught the tree and was drawn onto the full cock, and that when upon the ground a twig caught the trigger, and it went off whilst the barrel was close against his neck, for his head fell onto the end of the barrel.   Anyone may see the direction of the shot along the ground, and be convinced that I could never have fired off a gun in that position; and I hope, sir, you will take your men to the spot and examine it.   It can easily be known by the pool of blood.   This is simply my statement, and to which I have no objection to put my signature."

This was done, and the magistrates then ordered the court to be cleared.

When we were admitted again there was a great crowd in, and the chairman said -

"We are come to the determination of committing you both to prison upon suspicion, and we are sorry to say, that unless some very favourable circumstance should arise to make us alter our opinion, you will remain there until the next Assizes to take your trial. In the meantime, poor Sealey may be able to dictate some account tending to your benefit, but of which we are bound at present in justice to doubt. The clerk will make out your commitment."

At the next moment there was a great stir in the court, and who should come forward in breathless suspense, to ask the magistrates if his son was murdered - but my father. There was I, there was he. He loved me and I loved him; but I dared not confess myself his son; nor would he, I thought, have owned me. So he arrived just in time to see me committed to Bury gaol upon suspicion of being an accomplice in a murder. He did not know me. I was glad he did not.

It is unfortunate that the newspapers of the day seem to have failed to report this story. Working on the estimate of 1799, neither the Bury & Norwich Post, nor the Ipswich Journal has yielded any trace of this story within two years either way. This is not surprising. If it happened at all, it happened at some distance from Ipswich and Bury, the centres of publication. No charges had been brought at this point. Also, those directly involved were from the lower classes. Even when their offences and accidents were reported, their names often were not, though their employer would usually be named.

Chapter 5 ~ The Prison

There is a very queer sensation to a lover of liberty upon entering a gaol. He does not like it. He feels, perhaps for the first time the authority of law - the strong arm thereof, which shuts out the fine fields, the open sky, the voice of men and children, and the notes of birds. What, then, must I have felt? My joyous escape from the severity of Mr. Rogers' school to the gipsy's encampment was soon ended, and but that I thought that father felt ashamed of such a gipsy boy as me, I should like to have gone home with him.

There is, however, a very wide difference between the consciousness of suffering for a fault of which we know ourselves guilty in the sight of God, and the actual suffering for another of which we know we are not guilty. But I was in for it. Gibson and I were received with all the honour of suspected felons; but as we were not yet tried, and only committed under strong suspicion, we were not treated exactly as if we had yet received our condemnation or our punishment.

I felt, however, that even the discipline of a gaol was not so bad as that of being flogged every week because I did not know how to do a sum in arithmetic, or translate Horace and Virgil, and could not do them under terror and compulsion.

> This seems to us to be the least believable part of the story. There is no evidence to prove or disprove the tale, but it seems unlikely that the boy would have been held in gaol when no other children in the family were. Also, would he really have failed to be recognised by his own father, or deliberately allow himself to be sent to gaol rather than face being reconciled with his family?

I felt I had not been accessory in any way to the misfortune of the gamekeeper. I suffered in spirit, from the thought of the poor fellow. I suffered for Mog. I suffered for the gipsy wife and mother. I suffered most for the gipsy himself.

The privations were all his. Those men who have felt accustomed to the open air, feel much more confined, when they are shut up in a cell, than those who have all their lifetime been subject to a sedentary life.

I slept for the first night in a prison upon a mattress and bedstead, not quite so soft as the gipsy's straw, with clothing for my coverlet. My gipsy dress was taken from me, and a gaol dress put upon me. Passive obedience was my duty, and there I was, passive enough.

This was before the building of the new Bury Gaol in Sicklesmere Road. Prisoners were housed in a number of buildings. Females were kept in the Bridewell. What is now Moyses Hall Museum was the house of correction for convicted prisoners serving their sentences. The holding prison where Gibson and Steggall would have been held was at the left side of the Market Place as shown in the picture below.

72

Boy as I was, I saw that Gibson was unhappy. He did not seem comfortable, and days passed on, and no tidings came of our release; we began to fear that poor Tom Sealey was actually in such a state as to make recovery impossible.

It was, perhaps seven or eight days after our committal, that I missed Gibson from the courtyard where he was permitted to take exercise. I missed him greatly, and I learned that he was confined to his cell. I had seen the fine frame and friendly face altered, and I became alarmed lest he should be very ill. And ill he was.

I learned from the surgeon, and from the good chaplain, that Gibson was seriously ill. One day Gibson requested that I might be with him. It was complied with - and I went into his dormitory, where a chair was set at the end of the bed, that his long legs, which otherwise would have been out of bed, might be covered up. But, oh what a contrast in that long lank figure, now emaciated and worn in one week by dysentery and fever to a skeleton, and yet those eyes, now almost like a pair of globes sticking out from their sockets, and fixed upon me with a look of love and pity such as would shame anyone who could condemn him.

Poor Gibson! The spirit was alive in him, and when he looked at me, his words, though faint, were cheering.

"Boy, will you tell your own tale to the chaplain, or shall I?"

"Leave me to myself," said I; "Don't think about me - think only about yourself. I hope you will soon be better."

"So do I, my boy - but not in this world. No, my gipsy wanderings are over. Henry, I shall die where I am."

I burst into tears. I could not help it. I was not old enough to prevent it. My agony was too acute, and my heart too full. It was a boy's heart, and I felt as if I was about to lose the best friend I ever had. I have had noble friends since then; some who have given me the hand of uncommon politeness - some who have given me the hand of patronage - some who have given me the helping hand of pecuniary assistance, but the gipsy gave me the hand of friendship, and it was not the hand of a vagabond, or a man of this world, but the hand of a poor fellow who, but for my hand, would never have interested anyone beyond the prison walls. He gave me his hand.

"Boy," he said to me, "I am not a real gipsy. My name is not Gibson, but my wife's name was, and I took her name. She is of a gipsy tribe of the name of Hearne; but frequently they change their names. Her grandfather was a Gibson - her father was a Hearne, and I was -, I was -, a gentleman. Yes, boy, a great land owner in Surrey. My real name is Morris. I took my degree at St. John's Cambridge. I was the eldest son of Squire Morris of ___. I hunted with noblemen. I dined with gentlemen; I shot with squires, and I learned all the secrets of preserving pheasants, rearing foxes, drinking Burgundy and Claret - and so I might have done to this day if I could have swallowed but one golden pill, and have fancied that it did me good."

"And what was that, Gibson?"

"It was matrimony, boy, without love."

The Hearne family and the Smith family (Gibson's wife was buried under the name of Smyth) were two of the major gipsy families of the East of England. The Journal of the Gipsy Lore Society published an article by T.W. Thompson in the early 1900s (Vol XXIV), investigating this story. Though there clearly are discrepancies, and the names may not have been remembered correctly, there are cases of intermarriage between gipsies and gâjè (non-gipsies).

Poor Gibson requested me to help him to raise his head upon his pillow. I did so, and the poor fellow turned those bright eyes upon me, which were to shine but for a short time longer, yet then they did shine with a light so luminous that never did I behold the intensity of beauty in any eye so bright.

"Boy," said Gibson, "you are a gentleman's son, and can therefore appreciate a gentleman's story. The most difficult thing for any man to do is for a man of high degree to rejoice that he is brought low. Yet here am I, in a gaol, suspected of murder, and I never committed one, or thought of one, in my whole life. My parents, Henry, were wealthy, very wealthy, and lived on a beautiful estate near Croydon. I was sent to Eton College; yes, I, Gibson the gipsy, was the son of Squire Morris of ____, but now the family have removed to another family estate in Wiltshire. I was sent to St. John's, Cambridge; there I distinguished myself. But I came home after taking my degree, according to my parents' wishes."

This is a part of the story that it is very hard to validate. More than 50 years on, it is unlikely he would have remembered the names correctly. The gipsy claims to be Charles Morris, son of a rich landowner, and a student of Eton and St. John's College Cambridge. We are not sure of his age at this point, but he is probably rather older than the impression one gets from reading earlier chapters. Though similar names feature in the records of Cambridge University and Eton, they do not match this gipsy's story. He may have misled the young John Steggall. Steggall may have given a rather fanciful version of what was more mundane. Or, of course, the Reverend Richard Cobbold may have played a part in the creation of this unlikely, but romantic storyline.

"Fathers have a right to advise, but they have no right to compel a son to take the woman they please to be forever a companion. But my father was an absolute man - master of his wealth, master of my mother, master of his children; and he governed all by making them feel their dependence upon him for money.

There was a very highly respectable family, who lived in the same neighbourhood - Sir Charles and Lady Granger. They had an only child, certainly an accomplished and handsome person, not intellectual, but accomplished. She had a very high spirit, and was one of those commanding beauties who attract or command attention. She could not fail to be admired among all the young men of my own years and standing in society; but though I conversed with her, and danced with her, and dined with Sir Charles, and was favoured with many polite attentions, all of which I acknowledged with that respect which was due to their station in society, I had not the slightest conception or intention of paying that lady any more respect than the ordinary intercourse of society admitted of.

The first conscious blow to this composure of mind was given me just as I was one day about to go out pheasant shooting with my red and white spaniels. The servant came to me and said, 'My master, sir, desires to speak to you in his study.'

I went, gun in hand, into my father's elegant study, where were more books than he ever read, or ever thought of reading. I bowed respectfully, as I always did to him, and he treated me in the same respectful manner.

'You have done very well hitherto, my son, very well indeed; and had I been poor, your career would have been profitable to me and honourable to yourself. We are all justly proud of you, and I hope we shall all be prouder still. I do not intend you should be a bachelor, I intend to marry you to the finest lady in the land, and to give her such a dowry as shall make it worth her while to marry you. My desire is, that you propose to Sir Charles and Lady Granger's daughter. My intentions are to give you fifty thousand pounds; my wishes, that you go and tell Sir Charles so this very day; and I hope you will enter into my views for your happiness.'

I stood still, riveted, breathless, and scarcely knew what to say. I believe I trembled; I know I felt such a quivering in my soul, that had my spirit gone out of me, there could not have been a greater agitation. I turned pale - felt faint - and my whole heart sick.

'What is the matter with you, my son? Many a man would jump at my offer of fifty thousand pounds and a bride. I have told Sir Charles all about it. He says he likes you, and his daughter likes you, and what would you more?'

'Only that I liked her.'

'You conceited ass! Pray is it not enough to be aware that all things are arranged between us, and that nothing lies between you and honour?'

'Except, sir, the doing of one of the most dishon-ourable things in this world; the making an offer of your hand to a lady to whom you cannot give your heart.'

'Heart, boy, heart! Why not? Heart! Bah, Bah! You give her a handsome dowry, she is a clever woman, and what would you give her more?'

'Father, you would not have me marry her if I did not like her?'

'That I would, and trust to your liking her afterwards.'

'That I feel she never would do.'

'Why not?'

'Because I feel that I could not like her.'

'Humph! Then I insist upon your trying to like this young lady. I like her very much, and it is only a piece of mock modesty on your part; the most nonsensical thing I have heard of - absurd beyond all folly. I thought you knew the world too well to be so childish. You, a son of mine, and to be as faint and fickle about such a matter as a child! Go; go your way. Go and walk into the woods, and if you do not like fifty thousand pounds and Miss Granger, then take a rope with you into the heart of the wood and hang yourself.'

' No, father; I have too much regard for myself and you to be guilty of any such folly. I would not hang myself, nor would I do anything so abominable.'

'Well, I do not care what you do. If you thwart my counsel in this matter you may go where you will. I will do nothing for you.'

'It is not counsel, father, but absolute tyranny.'

'Dare you speak so to me, young man? Just march out of this room and never let me see your face again until you can think better of my offer.'

There are strange motives in the heart of man. I retired. My dogs jumped up with delight to see me and I was anxious to divert my mind. On I went towards the wood. Hares came bounding out of the wood, pheasants flew up and rabbits, woodcocks and partridges passed me by.

I took the footpath at the end of the wood leading across the fields, and arrived at another of our copses. On I went, meditating upon the best way to proceed.

Had my father given me fifty thousand pounds, and told me to make my own choice for life, then would he have been, as I hope many fathers are, of a noble mind, and one who loved the noblest independence of his child. But to tell me that I must take with that fifty thousand the woman of his choice, and not my own!

Not feeling disposed to go any further, I sat down upon the stump of an oak tree, resolved to come to some conclusion. How singularly do things happen! At that moment, I heard a female voice singing close by me in the lane, these very words:-

What is the world to the weary man,
And what is the world to me?
I can bid them defiance, deny it who can,
For I love to be joyous and free.

Though my lord in his mansion may proudly sit,
In the state of his pride, may be;
He cannot enjoy himself never a bit,
So much as a gipsy free.

Though the squire may ride o'er the country
round,
And dash through the coverts with glee;
Yet what are his hunters, and what is his hound,
To the gipsy so happy and free?

Though the Jew rolls in riches and revels in joy,
Yet what in the forest is he?
I had rather be poor with a gipsy boy,
And live with the lively and free!

Oh what is the world to the careful and proud?
At best but an old rotten tree;
I love not the bustle, I love not the crowd,
But I love to be happy and free.

Then give me no state, but contentment at home,
Let my heart with my own kindred be;
With my gipsy husband through forests I'd roam,
And we should be happy and free.

A joyous laugh, and 'Bravo, girl!' rang through the thicket, and presently a voice - 'Take care, Mog, the young squire may be out shooting and hear you.'

'And what care I if he is?   Do you think, father, I care
for the squire or anyone else whilst we do them no
injury?'

'Hush, chatterer, hush; I hear somebody in the wood.'

And in the next moment I was at the gate to see the
singer.   There was a motley group of gipsies, old and
young, a fire smoking in the lane, and two or three raw-
boned figures of men, and mothers and daughters, all sitting round the fire.   When I appeared the men rose and
paid their respects to me.

'Where is your singer?' said I.

'Here I am,' said she, and she jumped up and looked at me full in the face; but ah! Ah! Too bold that look to last. It was no doubt the spirit of her words, 'who cares for the squire?' that made her jump up to confront him; but the moment she saw me, that moment, strange to say, it told me she was not impudent, for the gipsy blushed and dropt a curtsy, and I was equally struck with her.

'Will you sing me that song again?' said I.

'Not today sir.'

'When, then, will you?'

'Tomorrow at the same time.'

'You will sing it then, to me?'

'I did not say so, sir.'

'What did you say?'

'I said I would sing the same song at this time tomorrow.'

'And not to me?'

'I will sing it, sir, tomorrow, whether you like to hear it or not.'

'I should like to hear it again.'

But the girl would not come to me, and was evidently afraid, notwithstanding all her boasting. I gave the father a crown, and never did song do my heart more good than that. I returned with a light step toward my father's house, and I verily believe, happier than I ever was in all my life.

When I met my father, it was with a spirit restored to equanimity, and much more consciously powerful in itself than it ever was. He gave me his hand, saying, 'Your walk has done you good?'

'Yes father, it has.'

'Come, come, I always said you were in the main a sensible young man, and though you have not obeyed me this day, in going and doing as I would have had you do, yet Sir Charles and his Lady will dine with us today, and Emily also. Your brother Robert will be here from town, and I hope you will yet come to your senses.'

'I am perfectly in my senses, father. I am glad my brother Robert is come, and I hope we shall all have a happy party.'"

Poor Gibson was greatly fatigued by his exertion, and would have fainted, but the doctor had granted, or rather ordered, a little brandy for him.

"Boy, pour out a little brandy into that glass. My spirit is more exerted to speak than my body will bear, and do not give me too much - only a little drop. I do not want much to sustain my stomach. There! There, that will do. Now listen again."

"That very evening my father had what we termed a family party. I was in most excellent, I might say, exuberant spirits, for well did I know in my own mind that the proud Emily had no peculiar charm for me above the ordinary routine of sociable intercourse. I was therefore perfectly easy in her company, and chatty, and lively.

My father sat thinking in his own mind that his fifty thousand pounds had won my affections. It certainly was a tempting bait, and many a very serious-minded man - yes, a very grave, quiet, wise, judicious, long-headed man - would have swallowed the hook. Lust of money blinds, love opens the eye, and, as the later was a principle in my head not to be bribed, I was uncommonly quicksighted for a youth, and had no intention of making an offer to the lofty Emily.

It was evident, however, that she expected it was to be so - in fact, she was given to understand it would be so. She, with a strange sort of coquetry, as if she would try to make me declare myself, played off a sort of game of hearts with my brother Robert. Brother Robert was won completely. My father became excessively fidgety, for although he had sent for Robert, yet he had determined I should be the man.

There never could have been anything more subtly managed altogether. Father was playing his game; Sir Charles and Lady Granger were delighted with me; Emily did not care for Robert; Robert was in love with her; and I was the most free of the whole party. I knew it - free from the snares of the temptation of fifty thousand pounds.

Emily sang one song that evening rather a home-thrust to me, and the more so from her unconscious thereof. It was -

The Gipsy of Ringwood

The Gipsy of Ringwood is merry and gay,
She laughs in her tent in the bright month of May,
And though brown is her face yet her eye is all bright,
For the Gipsy of Ringwood is airy and light.

She can tell me my fortune! She points to the hall,
And deceives the young maiden with love's winding thrall.
Oh! Believe not the Gipsy of Ringwood's deep shade,
Though she promise a lover to every maid.

But the Gipsy of Ringwood may tell thee a tale -
And if folly be thine, shall o'er folly prevail;
Oh! Mind not the gipsy - but keep thine own will,
And love thou the lover who loves thy love still.

I certainly admired the song more than I did the singer, and though very well sung, yet it wanted that thrill, that truth, and that true freedom of note which I heard in the wood. The thought came over my mind, could anyone be aware that I had visited the gipsies' tent, and could anyone have told her that I had asked a gipsy girl to sing to me, or that I was going on the morrow to hear one. Oh, no! It could not be; my secret was with myself. I praised the song. I believe I asked for it again. She complied, and I drew near, and looked at her so earnestly that, happening to turn my eye upward from her, who should I see looking at me, as I then thought with jealously, but my brother Robert.

'You admire that song, Sir?' she asked me.

'I do. There is something so pleasantly simple therein, it is very taking.'

'You admire perhaps a real gipsy fortune-teller more than the song of the Gipsy of Ringwood?'

This was a home-thrust again, and I felt the blush mantle on my cheeks, and she saw it, and thinking she had justly reproved me, she turned to my brother Robert and said -

'I hope you are not so barbarous, sir!'

'Most certainly not, Miss Granger; I prefer your song and the style in which you sung it to all the gipsies in Ringwood Forest.'

It was now my turn to have a little revenge.

'But, Robert, let me ask, do you not admire the singer a great deal more than the song or the subject of the song?'

And I turned away to speak to Sir Charles, leaving my brother, Robert, to make what comment he pleased upon the question, or to take what advantage he would. What he did say, I know not, but in another minute the lady was across the room to her mamma, and her mamma across the room to Sir Charles, and Sir Charles across the room to the bell, and my father across the room to both, urging them not to be in a hurry, but to wait supper.

But no! The servant came in.

'Sir Charles Granger's carriage!' And then there was an awkward sort of formal pause, as if something unexpected had happened.   I, of course, went forward to hand the ladies to their carriage. I offered my arm to the young lady, but she took her father's. I then offered it to Lady Granger. She took it, but with very great dignity.

Scarcely had I made my bow at the carriage steps, before my father's voice summoned me to his study.

'A pretty fool,' says he, 'have you made of yourself this evening.'

'Have I, sir? In what way?'

'In what way, sir! Why, in deceiving a lady into the idea that you were going to do what I ordered you to do in the morning, and then doing completely the reverse this evening.   Did I not insist on your making Miss Granger an offer?'

'Did I promise so to do?'

'Did you refuse so to do?'

'Yes I did.'

'And do you refuse still?'

'Yes I do.'

'Sir, do you know the consequence?   I vow that you shall know it! You may take your choice. Miss Granger and fifty thousand pounds, or no Miss Granger and beggary. I give you two days to consider the matter in. You either take my offer, or I discard you for ever.'

'But my brother Robert likes her.'

'That is no matter to me. I like that you should have her, and not Robert.'

'But if Robert tells me he likes her, would you be so cruel as to expect me to marry her?'

'I care nothing about Robert's likes or dislikes. My likes are better than all dislikes, therefore go your way; two days - two whole days - and my decision is made that upon your refusal to take my offer, I refuse ever to see your face again.'

I sought Robert. I ascertained the state of his heart. The fact was, Robert was all sincerity, and the lady all politeness. It wanted, I suspect, only the fifty thousand pounds to put them both right."

Chapter 6 ~ A happy Death

"The next day at breakfast there was a melancholy seriousness spread over the former happy countenances of the father and mother and brothers, as if there was going to be a great change among us all.

The will of a parent should be obeyed by a dutiful son; but the horror of conventional matches was so great upon my mind - and certainly my distaste to marry the lofty lady who was so wrapt up in herself was such - that Barbados, or the Antipodes, or even beggary appeared to me preferable.   Never do I remember the proverb coming home to me more forcibly than it did then - 'better is a dinner of herbs where love is, than a stalled ox and hatred therewith.'

Brother Robert was full of gloom and apprehension. Father and mother retired leaving Robert and me to ourselves.

'My dear fellow,' he said, 'What will you do?'

'Go to Barbados, Bob.'

'But have you any money?'

'I have enough; do not trouble yourself about me.'

'But what do you intend to do?'

'That I will not tell anyone.   My determination is to be independent of this matter and to take all the consequences.'

'Well, do not let me cause you to do anything rashly.'

'I am not a boy, Robert, to run away from a good home, as if I had done wrong; or as if I wanted to squander away my portion.   No; my object is to do something for myself, and I scarcely know what that something is. Time will show.   At all events, brother, you shall never hear any hurt of me, either towards yourself or to anyone else.   But come, will you go and shoot with me?'

'I cannot.'

'Then I shall go without you.'

And if the truth be told, I was more glad he did not go than if he had accepted my proposal; for I had a strange notion of my own, like a presentiment that something momentous was about to take place with regard to myself. So I bade him goodbye, and told him I should be home to dinner.

I took my gun. I would only have the spaniels, no bushers, for I had reasons of my own for going alone. My object was not shooting, as you know, but to hear the gipsy sing and speak.

I walked towards the wood at the very time appointed. Even before I reached the old oak stump I heard the voice - the same song, the unmistakeable freedom of which I admired so much the day before. If possible, it came with a greater thrill over my mind, because of the strange situation in which I was placed.

There stood I at the gate, and happening to turn my head, I saw the singer leaning on her mother's neck and looking after me. There stood Hearne, and never was a man more astonished than when he heard me say, 'Hearne, will you let me be a gipsy?'

'Let you be a gipsy, squire? What do you mean?'

'I mean what I say; aye, and I am so much in earnest, that I will give you fifty pounds to take me in.'

'Master, you are joking.'

'No such thing, Hearne - no such thing. I tell you why and wherefore I am determined to become a gipsy.'

'You cannot be one, squire.'

'And why not?'

'You are so well known hereabouts.'

'And can you not move?'

'Quickly.'

'Then the quicker the better. Will you take me in?'

'For how long?'

'For life.'

'That I cannot promise. But pray, squire, let me ask you again, what makes you so earnest in this matter?'

I told him all the facts. I told him my resolve, and he promised never to betray me.

'Well, squire, and when will you come?'

'This very night.'

'We will do our best.'

'And you will find I will do mine. I will contrive to be with you by nine o'clock. Get a gipsy suit ready for me. In all things make me conform to your habits; and have patience with me, and you will soon find me a brave gipsy.'

'I never was so confounded before; but I will see and arrange as well as we can. You make me marvel. I need not say, squire Morris shall be welcome; but you will find it a hard life - a great change.'

'Aye, Hearne, and for the better, not for the worse.'

That night I dined at my father's table for the last time.

After dinner, I proposed to go and change my dress. I did so; and when I came into the drawing room, poor Robert was lying on the sofa positively ill. His heart was almost broken within him.

'Brother Charles, don't go out tonight; I feel so bad.'

'You will feel better presently, Robert. Cheer up! Don't be melancholy.'

I knew what was the matter with him, and I knew he would soon be cured. He looked at me; aye, and the more earnestly, as I said, 'well, goodbye - I must be off.'

I left him. In less than an hour from that time, Henry, I had done as you did, trusted my life and fortune to a gipsy."

Here poor Gibson fainted and big tears rolled down his cheeks; but when he lifted up his eyes, they were orbs of light.

I was in prison, and locked in; I could only attend to his wants with such things as were within my reach; yet the attention of a child is a blessed thing, for a child is gentle and careful; so I put the little glass to his lips, and he smiled again, and I could see his emotions that made us both weep - he for his own, and I for him.

Gibson was revived, and resumed his story.

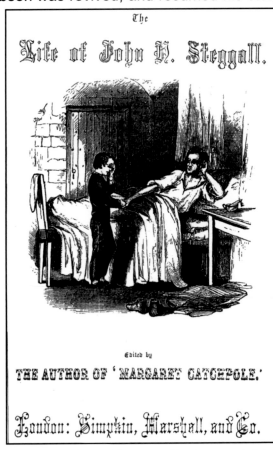

The title page from the first edition of what later came to be known as *'The Suffolk Gipsy'*

"I joined the gipsy, Hearne, that very night. Let it suffice, Henry, that I found them very kind and considerate

90

towards me, and you will see how I became such towards you. We went off that very night, and travelled into Kent, and never more was the eldest son of Squire Morris heard of, and never more, as such, is he likely to be. Much has been said against gipsies; they are many of them vagabonds; but the family I joined were a temperate and an industrious family. They treated me with the greatest respect, and I soon learnt to be independent and free. At first I had many severe trials, and none greater than a severe illness, in which the matron and the daughter nursed me as if I had been their own relative. I could never repay them for their kindness. I felt I never could. Yet I married Mog - aye, at the little village church of Barming; and I have ever found her the same active, energetic, and honest partner she promised to be. Volumes upon volumes might be written upon our career.

In Thomson's investigation into this story, mentioned earlier (Journal of the Gipsy Lore Society Vol XXIV) he is clear that there is no entry in the parish register for Barming in Kent that seems to tie up with this story. It is, after all, a strange detail to have been remembered over such a long time and is a likely embellishment at the time of writing. The Gipsy Lore Society set great store by the oral tradition and the remembered history of gipsies, collected around 1900. To this end, Thomson suggests that Steggall's story is basically true but very confused. He tells of how Paizi, youngest daughter of Francis Heron (or Hearne) was known to have married Anthony Hammond, a gentleman whose father had a landed estate in the South East of England. It is more than likely that this tale became interwoven with Steggall's own experiences.

Marriages between gipsies and non-gipsies, though uncommon, are recorded. In Howitt's 'Rural Life of England', there is mention of our story in reverse, where a gamekeeper's daughter married a man described as a member of the Boswell gang.

We separated from the others in the gipsy camp after some years and I came into Suffolk where I am well known. I have travelled over all the southern and eastern parts of England, and I could tell the histories of many of the families therein for a whole century. I, the gipsy, have passed all my days in peace. We have had many tempests, many shocks, many troubles; but my dear gipsy songster is worthy of a happier home than a prison. Many years have passed away, and now my days are shortening. I envy no one. I have been accustomed to luxury, to hardship, and to danger. But Mog and I have kept peace in our own hearts, and not until I opposed her daughter's marrying the gamekeeper, did I find my way into a prison.

But you must go and fetch my wife and daughter Mog. I am persuaded all will yet be right before I die."

Scarcely had these words been uttered before the door opened and the jailer announced our liberty. Poor Sealey had recovered his senses, and totally exonerated Gibson. He had become quite miserable - had sent for the squire - had begged of the clergyman to convey anything and everything he had to the gipsies, and an order for our immediate release had been signed. But it was too late - too late for poor Gibson ever to regain the fertile fields and lanes of Suffolk.

The name Gibson does feature in gipsy records, but mostly in the Northern parts of England at that time. Gibson described how the gipsies he knew used to regularly change their names. This seems to have been the case as both articles from the Gipsy Lore Society Journal, and local newspapers show gipsies at the time to have frequently been known by aliases.

I was soon sent on my gipsy errand to the camp at Norton. As may be supposed, I was not long in going;

for, thanks to the chaplain, jailer, and surgeon, there was,  even to me, as a poor gipsy, unjustly, though not unsuspiciously sent to prison, a generous feeling of regard. They sent me in a pony gig; for I was too young then to know the way, though it was but eight or nine miles off Bury. I made the boy stop at the bottom of the lane. I rushed into the gipsies' tent - Mog caught me in her arms. I cried with sorrow, and I cried with joy; but I said with vehemence -

"Haste, mother! Haste, Mog! - Go, both of you, this instant to Bury gaol; Gibson desires me to send you. He is ill, but he is free. Haste, mother, haste! I will not be long behind you. Go - go! The boy and gig are at the end of the lane, and we will follow you."

There was an earnestness in my manner and an eloquence upon my tongue, which needed no second hint. They were in the jailer's gig in an instant and off for Bury. Scarcely were they gone, and I had been telling all the sufferings of the father, before that good man, the Rev. Mr. H____, paid us a visit. He had been - as a good-hearted, generous, and humble Christian minister ever is - mindful of the souls of all in the gipsy encampment. He actually proposed to take us all in his family

This parson is something of a mystery. Hasted and Heigham were names of local parsons of the time, but our suspicion is that this refers to the prison chaplain, Rev. Rowland Hill.

van to Bury. Not only did he propose it, but he did it. I think I now see him driving up to the gaol with three gipsy sons, Jin, and myself, and to him we were indebted, all of us, for seeing the last of poor Gibson.

I must go back to the funeral of poor Gibson, which took place at Norton. It was a truly patriarchal scene. There was a composure, a firmness, a truly humble and heavenly resignation. That very day died poor Gibson the gipsy, alias Squire Morris, in the presence of his family, the two clergymen, and the runaway boy from the school of Mr. Rogers. It was a scene of affection such as I shall never forget. It was a lesson; one never to be erased from my mind.

St. Andrew's, Norton

There is no record of Gibson, or anyone from outside the parish of Norton being buried there at that time. Would one expect Steggall's memory to have let him down over this matter. It was, after all, the next parish to the one where he was later to minister for over 50 years. There are possible explanations. Maybe there was some kind of service with a burial elsewhere.

In her book, 'EAST ANGLIA - walking the ley lines and ancient tracks', Shirley Toulson reminds us of a piece of local folklore that places a gipsy grave beside the boundary oak along the Hundred Lane between Westhorpe and Badwell Ash. Could this have been Gibson's final resting place?

A final suggestion, (and it may be a complete red herring) but if Steggall was not present, he may have just got the wrong end of the stick. There is a village in Hertfordshire called Norton, well renowned for its gipsy graves. The Smiths, Mog's family, had connections in that area. Possibly, Steggall believed the Norton he had heard spoken of was the local village he knew and remembered.

I became a great object of attachment to the gipsy mother. Of course, she found that I knew all her history. She was very kind to me; but it was owing to that good clergyman that I was made to confess who I was. He undertook to see my father, and to reconcile him to me.

By this, we assume he means the Reverend Clerke of Norton. The marriage (over page) presents something of a difficulty, as does the true identity of this Tom Sealey. There is no record of a Tom Sealey (or Seely) marriage any time close to 1799. Terence Lee, in researching the Smith Gipsy Genealogies (privately published, 1995) suggests ways by which the gipsy Smiths may have been the key to this story, and that many names such as Gibson and Morris are to be ignored. Terence Lee has attempted to construct a family tree that makes sense of the story, but placing the shooting of the gamekeeper and the subsequent marriage several years earlier. The suggestion is that whilst Steggall may have spent time with the gipsies, he only learned the gamekeeper story round the camp-fire, perhaps even coming to believe, in the fullness of time that he had been part of it. However, we still find problems with this genealogy and have, at the end of this book, attempted to show the Seely family as revealed by parish records.

He did so.   He did more: he was instrumental in marrying Mog to young Sealey, in settling the Gibsons in
different situations, and in persuading Sealey to take
Mog's mother under his protection.

Who was Tom Sealey?

Thomas Seely married Susan Osborn around 1781. They
had at least five boys and five girls, most of whom were
baptised at Finningham, including a boy called Thomas in
1782. He died ten years later, and four years after that, in
1796, another Thomas was baptised at Finningham.

It is likely that Susan Seely (nee Osborn, Orsbourn,
Osborne etc.) came from Norton. The family long had a rep-
utation for dabbling in witchcraft and featured in newspaper
articles and local folklore. A number of them feature in the
overseers' accounts for Norton, as several Osbornes were in
receipt of parish relief.

Thomas Seely, born 1796, married Sophia Fletcher at
Norton in the winter of 1817. He was a blacksmith. They had
at least nine children.

We have burials recorded for just two adult Tom Seelys in
the area. Yet a third died and left a will. The burial of Tho.
Seely, labourer (47) at Finningham in 1808 is possibly the Tom
Seely mentioned first in this piece. Another Thomas Seeley,
buried at Finningham in 1884, aged 90 is almost certainly the
blacksmith who had been married to Sophia. So who was the
Tom Seely of Finningham who died and left a will in 1823?
Though it has been impossible to trace his burial, a will was
proved and received probate in June 1823, stating the date of
his death as April 6th 1823. The chief recipient was Susan,
his wife. This could lead one to believe **this** one was the husband of Susan Osborn. If that was the case, could the labourer who died in April 1808 be the missing gamekeeper? That
would seem unlikely, as Steggall talks later of visiting the
couple at their cottage after he had gone to sea, and his return
would have been after that date.

A will without a body is unfortunate to say the least. Perhaps the Tom Seely who died in 1823 had a non-conformist funeral, the records of which no longer survive. Or a gipsy funeral?

This 1823 will was meant to have been executed by one John Norman whom, it appears, died before the will could be proved. The most likely candidate for this would be John Norman (62) who was buried at Walsham in 1818. The burial register says he was from Finningham.

And more, he saw me placed at school, under a very different tutor, at the very school where Lord Ellenborough was educated, at the Rev. Mr. Hepworth's of Botesdale, who was a good and kind-hearted man, and very different to my former cruel master.

This is the remarkable building at Botesdale that is known as St. Botoph's Chapel. (Botesdale is a corruption of 'Botolph's dale') This building onced served as the Grammar School, attached to which was the Master's house.

Chapter Seven ~ The Sea

My return home was hailed with joy, as my parents had suffered very great anxiety on my behalf. The uncertainty of my condition, whether alive or dead, was the continual subject of conversation with them. Mr. Rogers' school, too, had suffered severely since my departure; for his was not like those great foundation establishments, where masters are provided for by endowments, which raises them above such fluctuations of pupils.

> Mr. Rogers' school continued until his death in 1807, his wife Frances dying the following year. As earlier stated, both boys and girls continued to be educated by their son Arthur and daughter Rebecca.

How different the character of Mr. Hepworth to whom I was now sent. He perceived in a moment that I was a boy of tender and delicate sensitiveness, and ill treatment was not the way to make me apply. He had heard, also, of my stay among the gipsies, and he took pleasure in cultivating my mind. In one year I gained more knowledge than in all former years and that which I gained I retained. My classical studies were then a pleasure.

But let not the reader imagine that my memory could ever forget the gipsies. No. There was a species of independence, or rather self-dependence, then taught me, which no scholastic tuition could destroy; and all my reading did but increase that ambition to do something for myself. Useful to a certain extent I had already been; experienced to a certain extent I had already become; but there still burned within me a longing desire to do something in the world. But no more runaways for me.

During the years I was with Mr. Hepworth, religion was made a practical, rather than a theoretical study; for the good man always encouraged cheerfulness, and used to say, 'Be good boys, and you will be happy men. Be kind to your parents and friends, and you will be likely to prosper in life. Study now, and you may take it easy hereafter.'

The street through Botesdale has changed little since John Steggall was a boy there

Yet we used to play in Redgrave park, and to fish, and to have our cricket in Barley Birch; to hurrah at the stage coaches, as they drove up to the Crown, and brought us the news of the stirring times of the French Revolution; and we had holidays for loyalty, holidays for victory, holidays for the King's birthday, and, of course, for our good old master's, on which day we had sumptuous fare and heart-felt fun.

The Reverend Hepworth of whom Steggall speaks so fondly is referred to in an item in the Bury & Norwich Post in October 1791 as the Schoolmaster at Botesdale Grammar School. His love of a good celebration is borne out by an article in the same newspaper in June 1794 stating that to acknowledge Lord Howe's victory over the French fleet, he provided strong beer for the men of Botesdale and organised feasting amid the firing of guns.

I was a lively boy, and though I had gone through heavy-hearted scenes, yet I was to go through many more before my grey hairs should arrive.

I was in a few years articled to a surgeon practising at Bacton. Here I had to make myself useful, to mix up medicines, hold men's heads, legs, and arms, and to bind up wounds. Craniology was not then a study, nor Phrenology, but limbs had to be set, teeth drawn, pills made, and of course swallowed, and many to be cured of various complaints; but nervous disorders, and rich fat farmers, and their wives and daughters, were all our best subjects in the Esculapian profession.

At that time, whilst Suffolk could boast a few doctors with formal medical training at the Royal College of Surgeons in London, for example, many trained by apprenticing themselves to local practitioners, in the way Steggall describes. It is unlikely he ever completed his apprenticeship. If we assume he left school no earlier than 1804, he probably served no more than three years at the most.

The surgeons at Bacton seem to have been as follows:

William Stearn - details in the overseers accounts show he worked there from about 1765 until at least 1784, and possibly a good deal longer.

An advert placed in the Bury Post in November 1808 announced that **Mr. S. Denny,** surgeon had taken over the premises previously in the occupation of **Mr. Pretyman,** trusting that he could rely on the previous surgeon's custom. It seems likely that this Mr. Pretyman may have been the surgeon to whom the young John Steggall was apprenticed. His departure may have been part of the reason for Steggall's change of life-style.

I had an old uncle, a clergyman, rector of Westhorpe, who took a great fancy to me. He was an old bachelor, my mother's brother, and he lived at Walsham, whither I often went, rode his horses, and sung many a cheerful song. Ah! They were apparently happy days. He had paid for my apprenticeship. He had found me money to walk the hospitals, but he always wished me to go to sea.

As can be seen from the Steggall genealogy at the end of this book, this would have been the Rev. John Heigham, uncle to John Steggall's mother, Mary. Whilst rector of Westhorpe until his death in 1812, he continued to live and act as perpetual curate at nearby Walsham-le-Willows, paying John Steggall's father Charles to serve as curate at Westhorpe. Charles Steggall came to have the rectory at Westhorpe as well as adjacent Wyverstone from 1812 on John Heigham's death.

"Boy!" He used to say to me, "your spirit should see the world. I wish you would learn to be a sailor. There's nothing like the joy of the free ocean, a stiff breeze, a good ship, and an open sea. Why not go on a voyage in one of my ships? You will see something of the world, and then, if you do not like it, you can but leave it."

My great chum at home at this time was my sister Peggy, as I used to call her. She went with me to pay a visit to Mog, whom I found as happy as ever I saw a woman in my long life.

Unfortunately, we do not know the real name of Mog, the gipsy daughter. It may be short for Margaret, but more than likely, she adopted her own mother's nickname in childhood, and her own Christian name may have been something entirely different.

Her aged gipsy mother was living with her. They had become completely civilised, if I may so term it, and more than that, she was a Christian in her heart; she was buried by me at ninety-five years old, at Westhorpe, forty years since. As may be supposed, she was glad to see me, though she could hardly recognise in the handsome young surgeon the dirty runaway schoolboy.

This reference to the burial of the gipsy mother is the one piece of firm evidence we have of the gipsy part of the story. Better still, as he knew he had written the evidence himself in the burial register for Westhorpe, he knew better than to elaborate on it and here we have something we can really rely upon.

Written in the Westhorpe register and clearly dated April 21st 1826, is written... *'Matthew Smyth a gipsey woman & mother of Gipsey Will.'* Written below in the same hand... *'1000 People attended the funeral.'* This is lightly crossed out. In the column marked **Abode**, is written *'Westhorpe Lanes Buried 8 feet deep,'* with all but the word *'Westhorpe'* crossed out. Old Mog's age is given as *'92 years'* and the minister's signature is that of *'Jn ⁿ Steggall.'* As Steggall was only serving as temporary curate at the time, we can assume that his rector felt he was entering up more than was strictly necessary. Large attendances at gipsy funerals were common, and some-times reported in local papers, especially when they ran up bills at local hostelries, only to melt back into the countryside the next day. In this case, however, we have been unable to trace any such report.

The age of Mog makes it almost impossible for her to have been the mother of the children described with her and Gibson. The mention in the register of Mog having been mother of Gipsy Will is an interesting one. He was a colourful character about whom much was spoken and plenty written. If Steggall had wanted to romanticise this story, why did he miss the opportunity to bring into the tale a character like Gipsy Will? Perhaps in his wish to show the gipsies in the best possible light, he drew a veil over such connections.

"You have left the life of a rover, sir," she said to me.
"No, Mog, no. You know me to be an active spirit. I am the youngest son of my father, and my uncle is fond of the sea. He has persuaded me to take a berth in one

of his vessels bound for the South Pacific Ocean, and as he has some property, and talks of providing for me, I think it best to let my father see I am disposed to ease him of myself, and not be a burthen."

"Well, well, sir, I am glad you are not truanting again. My dear mother lives with me, my husband is kind to me, and my brothers and Jin respect me, so I rejoice, dear sir, that you do not again run away from any ill treatment."

"Thank you, Mog - thank you. I almost envy you. But I have a desire to go to sea; and, if I do not return prosperous, I shall have gained, perhaps, a little experience of this wide, wide world."

"Pray, sir, will you condescend to write to me?"

"Oh yes Mog; and if I sometimes remind you of our gipsy days do not be surprised. Dear sister Peggy, remind me that I enclose a letter for Mrs. Sealey in my letters to you."

It was a truly nice neat little cottage in which the wife of Tom Sealey lived. He was out with the squire, and as I thought Squire N_____ would not be angry, I determined to drive round by the hall, and pay my respects to him. At all events, I should see the pleasant face of his lady.

I drove to the Hall. My sister and myself were admitted, and when I made myself known to the lady as the gipsy boy to whom she gave the penny, she was very much pleased.

She asked me of my fortunes and my views in life, and, going to a little bureau of hers, she brought forth a very pretty little present of a pocket compass, and wished it might be of some future service to me.

I took my leave of the kind-hearted lady. I told her I would take care never to jump into a lane again without looking before I leapt, and, desiring my respectful remembrances to the squire who had lashed me and committed me to prison, I departed. I soon took leave of my own family and friends, and went with my uncle to town. He got me my outfit, and put me on board his ship 'Adventure,' which was going upon a voyage for the purpose of whale fishing.

Though I afterwards saw lots of blubber, yet there was no blubbering with me then. I was committed to the care of Captain Moon, as second mate, and soon sailed down the river. For the first time I was upon the sea, and it was indeed an adventure.

The man they called Gipsy Will

Probably the man most responsible for bringing the Romany world to the masses was George Borrow. Travelling throughout Europe, he wrote of the people he met and the sights he saw, but, he did not always get it right any more than John Heigham Steggall did.

In his book, 'The Zincali', he writes at length about Gipsy Will, whom he describes as an arranger of prize-fights, a horse-thief, maybe even an accomplice in murder. He states that he was just fourteen, and within a league of Newmarket when he first encountered Gipsy Will.

"...I have still present before me his bushy black hair, his black face, and his big black eyes fixed and staring. His dress consisted of a loose blue jockey coat, jockey boots and breeches; in his hand was a huge jockey whip, and on his head (it struck me at the time for its singularity) a broad-brimmed, high-peaked Andalusian hat, or at least one very much resembling those generally worn in that province. In stature, he was shorter than his more youthful companion, yet he must have measured six feet at least, and was stronger built, if possible. What brawn! - what bone! - what legs! - what thighs!"

Unfortunately, Borrow goes on to say that Gipsy Will was hanged at the age of fifty in front of Bury Gaol, being executed with two others for a murder committed in his youth.

This clearly was innacurate as no such character was hanged in Suffolk. Gipsy Will was implicated in an earlier murder case that sounds remarkably similar to the one George Borrow mentions. Edmund Thrower was hanged in Ipswich in 1812 for a murder committed in Cratfield nineteen years earlier. Though the witness, John Head, spoke of Gipsy Will & John Saunders being involved (Saunders was a common alias used by the Smiths), neither was indicted on this occasion. The name William Smith (a gipsy) cropped up again in 1827 when three horse thieves were arrested at Westhorpe for a crime committed in Hertfordshire and transported to Van Diemen's Land later that year, but further investigation shows this Gipsy Will was too young. Thompson's previously mentioned article in the Journal of the Gipsy Lore Society (Vol: XXIV) found evidence to show that Gipsy Will remained in this part of the country, dying around 1850 at 'a good age.'

I am aboard - I am bounding with full sail down the channel, and bidding farewell to the scenes of old England, but not to all associations connected therewith.

My young hopes were then confined to the discharge of my duty to my uncle: and, of course, to the worthy skipper, Captain Moon.

"Young one," he said to me, the very first day I went on board, "you have everything to learn, and you have something to do. Make a friend of that old veteran with his pigtail hanging half a yard down his back, and he will soon teach you every part of the ship and the use of all the tackling aboard. He's a rough diamond, but many a diamond before it is polished may possess intrinsic value, so does that old seaman, John Crocket. - Jack, ahoy!"

Jack came and stood before the Captain.

"I've a young landsman here, appointed second mate, Jack; he is a bit of a surgeon, and he'll keep you in good health, if you will take him in tow."

"Aye, aye, master! What's your name, younker, I beg pardon, sir? Well, I don't care, I'll give you a name if you'll accept it. I always begin my pupils by giving them a name, and, as you say you're a bit of a surgeon, I shall call you Tom Pill, and you may call me Old Crotchet if you please, but John Crocket is my right name.

Come along Pill! Come along; we shall have some talk about the ship. I hope you are an apt scholar, for I never like telling a man the same thing twice over."

I remember the first lesson he gave me was about the wales.

"Boy," says he, "we are going to catch whales, but you ought to know that every ship has wales. Now look ye here: you see these stout timbers just above the water-mark of the vessel; these are called the wales, and ours in the Adventure are stout enough; you won't forget that?"

"Never."

It would take a long time to go through his lessons, upon fore-mast, main-mast, and mizzen-mast; shrouds, halliards, gangway, hawser, keel, jib, and jib-boom; spanker-boom, poop, ports, yards, waist, truck, tiller, tampion, taff-rail, ratlines, pawl, rudder, rowlock, keelson, hold, grapplings, gunwale, clewlines, buntlines, hull, hulk, stowage, and all things necessary to be understood. By little and little, I became master of the thing, and found Jack Crocket, though a rough seaman, a very rational one. Character as he was, he was as kind a hearted old fellow as ever lived. I shall never forget missing stays once and going plump overboard, but it was calm weather, and Jack's eye was upon me. I was coming down the shrouds, and thought to spring nicely on deck, just to show Jack how active a sailor I was becoming, when my foot caught the gangway, and over I went into the sea, and down to  the bottom I should have gone, but for Jack, who sprang over like a Newfoundland dog, and gave me such a gripe of the hair, that he lifted me up fairly out of the water, just as a man would hold a cod-fish by his gills.

A little later than this, from 1835, ships and their commanders were well recorded. As early as this (around 1808-9 -- he says it was 1807, but it was probably slightly later), records are more patchy, some muster rolls surviving. Though he does not say where they sailed from, he later speaks of returning to the Thames, so we assume the departure dock would have been somewhere like Greenwich or Chatham, unless of course, he embarked at Ipswich which was known throughout the eighteenth century as a whaling port.

We were bound for New Zealand, and to the South Sea. Our object was to get a full cargo of Spermaceti oil;

and our work, as anyone may imagine, was arduous. In the year 1807, the whole ocean was traversed by ships of war; privateers roamed in every sea, and yet our little ship of five hundred tons had to plough that immense ocean alone. We were adventurers indeed; rovers, it might be termed; for our captain and commander was the most thoroughly independent and noble fellow a sea-man can imagine.

He was strict in his discipline, steady in his conduct, and endowed with great presence of mind. Indeed, I saw him under all trials, aboard and ashore; and never was a man more master of himself and consequently, master of his men. And what gave him this authority? It was not bluster - I never heard him use an oath in my whole voyage with him. He was a temperate and sober man; a man of great intelligence, though he never attempted to show off, or ever pretended to know more than his duty.

As to me, I loved him as I did anyone and everyone who gave me instruction with generosity, and I do not think we had a man on board who did not do the same.

We had only twelve men - the Captain, coxswain, two mates and a cook, and our vessel was not one of the lightest in the world, with three great whale boats on board, and harpoons, cordage, knives and guns, mus-kets, anchors, grapplings, barrels, and various goods for the natives of the islands.

We were also to be prepared in case of pirates, as we should most likely traverse the western coast of Africa, so that we had guns, nets, pikes, pistols, swords, and weapons which we all hoped we should never have occasion to use.

Many men go aboard a ship with pain and regret, the same as boys go to school, and are never happy until they get home again. It was not so with me. If our skipper had his venture in the Adventure, I had mine. His was to give satisfaction to his employers; mine was to give satisfaction to both him and my uncle, by gaining all the information I could, and learning to do my duty in my new station of life.

We will pass over swabbing decks, furling sails, keeping watch, the different bells, and all the nautical minutiae of ship-board. We had a very small complement of men for a vessel of so many tons, and for such work as ours; but every man was a seaman and well paid, and glad to get employment in service at a distance from the war; but where was that in that day? All sailors who could be pressed were required for the king's service, so that we were fortunate to get away as we did, and to be on our voyage as we were.

To me, everything belonging to the ship was interesting. For I was just eighteen, the right age to be useful, and the right age for activity. I felt an affection for every man on board, and could describe all their characters, and features as well, so that if one of those men be now alive, he could not fail to recognise himself and his companions.

We were very fortunate on our outward-bound voyage, not meeting with a single mishap. We had storms, and the first I shall never forget, for having just recovered from my sea sickness, it was something so terrific to my young imagination, that after the lapse of nearly sixty years I can scarcely forget it. Well may it be said that seamen behold the grandeur of the elements. Men who stand on shore, and see the dashing of the sea, or the distant foam, can form no idea of the bounding action of a vessel driven in a storm under bare poles, up to the heavens, down again to the deep - up again and down again! On, on, on - perhaps a whole day and night, sometimes for two days together, and without the slightest lull.

I love to see the ocean lively - I love to see a brisk breeze and all things in motion; but the first storm at sea filled me, I confess, with the most awful consternation. The more I saw of the fearful sky and the mighty waves, the more I thought of the utter insignificance of man, and yet, there we were, helpless indeed, the captain at the helm, myself at his feet, holding the speaking trumpet for him, and clinging with one arm to the lashings which kept both him and myself to our posts.

This voyage is difficult to substantiate with any degree of confidence. The registers of Lloyds of London list two ships from this time named *'Adventure.'* Neither was listed as a whaler. Both were brigs: one of 200 tons had been built at Whitby in 1780, the other of just 74 tons was built in 1801 in France. The earlier ship did operate out of Greenwich, and had been to the Southern hemisphere, transporting convicts. It is quite likely it could have been refitted for whaling. However, Steggall describes a 500 ton ship. But he also names a crew of twelve, plus the captain, which seems far too few for such a venture.

It would have been impossible for me to have stood upon my feet, I should have been blown away in an instant; sails we had none; even the cordage flew about and how the beams bore the straining was to me a marvel.

Chapter 8 ~ Bird Fishing and Whaling

The Adventure moved onward with various winds; catching our first view of the coast of America off Rio Janeiro after five weeks' voyage. We stood off land, however, and continued our course, passing through the latitude of Rio de la Plata.

The old Adventure was not easily blown away; though a heavy ship, she was a steady one: such too was the character of her jolly men on board. We experienced very variable winds along this coast. One hour perfectly calm - another 'right in our teeth' - another cast us on our beam-ends - then we had a noble scudding before the wind.

One morning I remember standing near the bows, with Old Jack Crotchet as he was called; it was the 4th of April, the wind being a light south-easter, when I saw heavy clouds apparently travelling along the horizon; and driving, as it were, in an opposite direction to our vessel. I said to old Crotchet, "Look yonder! The clouds are all running a race," for they appeared to be going one over the other, as if they had started to see which could drive the fastest.

Old Jack called out in an instant, "Furl all sails, brace up the yards. Tom Pill, call the Captain!"

This was done in a moment; and when the skipper came, Jack pointed to windward; and that was enough.

"Now, my boys, up with you," said Captain Moon. "Furl up the mizzen-top; slacken the lee main-topsail braces; put the helm to starboard. Wait a bit - steady!" And in one moment, down came the squall, away went the ship at the rate of ten knots an hour; and every man seemed to enjoy the run. It was a run; for what the clouds had been doing in the morning, we were doing all the day, playing a game of racing with the waves. In this way we passed the Falkland Isles; and though the gale abated, yet we were prepared, with getting in the flying jib-boom, for the bad weather off the Cape.

But we passed the Cape, keeping our course still to the south, towards New Shetland, that mass of coral rocks between which and New Zealand lay our enterprising search for whales.

Of New Shetland we knew nothing; all I remember it by, was, because the first fishing we had for birds happened to be there.

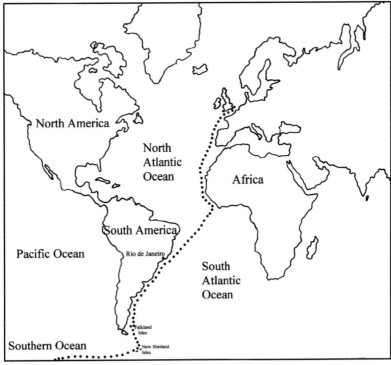

Yes, fishing with hook and line for birds seems a curious thing for a sailor, especially for whale-fishers. But the sailors were all permitted to try their luck; and, as we were surrounded with what they call Cape pigeons, a little sea fowl of a fishy, but not unsavoury taste, we had great success.   These pigeons followed our ship, and kept flying, and swimming, and skimming around us, and were attracted by any bit of meat, fish, bread, or anything white and glittering.   A hook baited with a bit of fish was the best lure, and we caught sufficient to make a capital pie, of which we partook voraciously.

But our fishing was not always for what we could eat. One bird which we often saw in this latitude, was the silent and beautiful companion of our comparative solitude.   I sometimes dream, even now, that I see that ghost-like bird, sweeping in his majestic flight along the trough of the sea; like some airy phantom of the brain. Yet as I looked at it, it reminded me of my dear sister Margaret and home.   It was something pleasant to have a noble creature, white as a virgin bride, sailing along

Steggalls's tale of this trip is full of colour and accurate in its detail. His Cambridge University biographical sketch accepts this part of the story as accurate. The one doubt we have is the timing of his book. It was written at a time when whaling stories were at their most popular. 'Moby Dick' by Herman Melville had been published under the title 'The Whale' in 1851, as had William Kingston's famous yarn 'Peter the Whaler.' Sounding remarkably familiar to the albatross story in Steggall's book, this extract is from William Kingston's novel, 'The South Sea Whaler.' It is not the only similarity.

'*Before long, a huge white albatross, with wide-extended wings, which had been hovering about the ship, espying the bait, darted down and swallowed it at a gulp, hook and all. In an instant it was secured, and the bold seaman came running in along the yard to descend on deck; while the bird, rising in the air, endeavoured to escape. Its efforts were in vain; for several other men aiding Hulk, in spite of its struggles it was quickly drawn on board. Even then it fought bravely, though hopelessly, for victory; but its captor despatched it with a blow on the head.*'

with us in those solemn seas, and though not speaking directly to us, yet evidently catching its food as we disturbed in our course the shoals of fish through which we drove.

But I little thought we could hook an albatross. When we think of a silent pair of wings, fourteen feet from tip to tip - no swan in England ever measured such a length.

"I'll show you how to catch that bird," said Jack; "Look here, Mr. Pill, do you see this lump of salt-junk made soft by boiling? Yon fellow will bounce at it like a hawk, when it dashes out of the spray of our ship. Look

Albatross

sharp now; throw you the line out a-head upon the wave, so that we give the line a jerk just as we make way through the crest of the wave, but not long before I point out the majestic bird coming with his long swoop alongside our ship. Look out, look out, here he comes! Out with it."

And I hurled it as far as I could with the wind, and presently we came up to it. We dashed it aloft with the jerk of the string, and the bound of the vessel on the crest of the wave, and it was instantly seized and as instantly swallowed by the noble albatross, who in another instant received such a check as turned him over on his back, and he fell directly upon the sea.

I never saw him till that moment off the wing: but he was flying again in a moment - then again chucked down. He was hooked, poor fellow, fairly or unfairly hooked, and afforded much sport to the sailors, by his incessant efforts to escape.

Vain was it for him to fly. He dropped upon the ocean, and for a while he rode majestically along our side with his beautiful neck outstretched and his mouth wide open, endeavouring in vain to disgorge the hook from his throat, till, nature fairly exhausted, the poor bird could struggle no longer, but was drawn up on board and laid upon the deck, just in time for us to see him die.

So it was, to my mind, that that noble bird died upon the deck of the Adventure. I was permitted by the Captain to skin the bird, and I preserved it. I afterwards had it stuffed, and presented it as a present to my sister Margaret.

We wore off those volcanic islands, the New Shetland, which were but little known, when it was proposed to go and catch some seals. The whole coast, at that time, abounded with them, and we were as much a subject of curiosity to them as they to us.

Seals of the world from *'Goldsmith's Animated Nature'*

These islands had been visited by very few navigators, being much out of the latitude of those who weather Cape Horn for the purpose of visiting the western coast of South America. So seldom had a boat approached the shore, that all animated nature seemed to be sporting in the joyousness of existence, without thought of danger.

There were seals in every attitude imaginable; some were seated with dignity upon a ledge of rock, and looked almost human; others were diving into the flood; others bathing as if at play, like schoolboys in those days of fun and frolic, when they visit the bright waters amidst schoolfellows of their own age and try their prowess in the stream. Beside our boat millions of little fish were swimming, and we had no difficulty in catching thousands.

And now commenced our work of slaughter. The first gun we fired was at an immense seal who stood up out of the water like a human being, come up from the mighty deep to look at us, and certainly not the oar's length from the boat. We had immense swan shot, so that, when this curious looking animal, indulging his first glance at man, thought us friends, he little expected to receive such a salutation. He turned over, and over, and over, completely unsensed by the number of shot entering his brain, so that he was captured, a dead seal directly. His bulk was enormous. He measured eight feet from the head to the tail, and was six feet in circumference. He was soon hauled in and stowed away in our deep-sea whale boat.

What with birds, and seals, and fish, we returned to the ship loaded, so that we had not time to go ashore, if we could have done so. Seamen without some kind of sentiment about them are very indifferent about scenery.

Some of them, indeed, take delight in doing anything for their comrades who are curious about things, and as I was fond of shells, corals or birds, and always had a turn for curiosities, many of them took delight in bringing me even a particular sea-weed, or shell, or fish, so that I had a complete museum of our expedition.

However much I had to rough it, I never failed to see, with heartfelt astonishment, beyond all that I could express, the living wonders of the deep; and though an active youth, my mind was so singularly reflective, that I do not think a single thing, from the mast-head of the vessel to the keel, from the tip of the bowsprit to the rudder, ever passed my eye without reflection.

Another boat's crew went to the Shetland rocks, and, I believe went on shore, but I was not appointed this time, so that I can only say they brought us home plenty of fresh fish and fowl. I had to attend to a poor sick sailor, and as I acted as assistant surgeon to the ship, I had not my name Tom Pill for nothing. When the boats came alongside, and were again hauled up with all their provisions, Captain Moon set sail for the South Sea. We presented a rather curious sight on board. What with seal-skins hanging about to dry, and our birds hanging up, and portions of flesh drying as well, it was fortunate for us that we encountered no rough weather.

We were now fairly within the Antarctic Circle, and had to contend with floating ice continually. I may as well name that open space into which we sailed in latitude 65 degrees south and longitude 120, when the cry from the mast head was, "fish ahoy!" I remember running up the rigging to have a look into that bay. It was not a bay inland, but a bay in ice - an ice-bound bay - and a romantic, fairy-looking scene it was, compared with that which we had been traversing.

The impression now upon my mind is that of a vast

field of waters, surrounded by a white and shining fringe of sometimes maiden whiteness, sometimes rosy tinged, sometimes, or in some places, purple, with here and there indented spots, like distant caverns. This vast amphitheatre of miles, was a lively scene to a sailor's eye, and especially to the whale-fisher. To me, who had never seen such a scene before, it was as extraordinary as new. In parts, those mountains rose with spiral grandeur into the heavens, and then again seemed as if they had been by some art of man cut down into a long flat plain, and then to rise boldly up again, and so to cir- cumscribe a vast field of water, within which lay the unconscious objects of our long search.

There lay the creatures of the deep; the leviathan whose histories I had read of in my boyhood, but never expected to behold. There they lay - I did not count their numbers. Some were sailing quietly along as if guided by a rudder, and looked like the bottom of a ship, moved by the wind and waves after being capsized; others were spouting forth a column of froth and water, which was intended, probably, to clarify their great mouths of many things that had inadvertently got foul of their immense fibrous range of seam-like teeth; for the whale always swims with his mouth open, and captures everything that chances to come within the vortex of his eddy, and he only closes his mouth when he sends forth that tremendous blast of waters from his conical volcano.

All was life and animation on board our ship. Preparations were quickly made. All the various officers and men belonging to the ship's company were aroused, and the busy sailors soon unhanked the boats, and every man seemed to take to his duty. Harpooners, boat-steerers, line-managers, carpenters, coopers; all now were in and at their proper work.

The boat was lowered, and manned with a complement of six for the oars, and a harpooner and rope-coiler, and steersman, and away we went. I was in the boat, and old John Crocket by my side.

We proceeded in a line about a mile from the ship, and, from what I could see in the boat, the whale lay perfectly unconscious upon the waters until the boat drove directly upon it; and then instantaneously received the harpoon into its back. One immense splash I saw, and it disappeared. We joined on a second line of 120 fathoms, and still the line ran on to about a third of our own second line, and then there was for a moment a lull; but again it ran on.

In about a quarter of an hour, the monster came up, puffing or blowing into the air, a stream of water as if enraged, until, at length fairly exhausted, the immense creature lay upon the waters to have our long spears thrust into his vitals, and then he turned upon his back and died.

I remember if I did feel pain at the death of the first whale, it was excitement, enterprise, sagacity, the conquering of danger, and a sense of duty to my employer, which made me ardent and active.

It is not for me here to describe the various processes of skinning, cutting up, packing the blubber in casks, and tearing out the long fibrous teeth for the whale-bone. Our object being oil, the flesh is taken no notice of, and the blubber or fat, which is the only part we look upon as valuable, is of sufficient consistency to be cut up after being hauled on board into long slips, and so thrust into the bung hole of a cask.

After we had 'flensed' the whale, which took us six hours, we pursued others, and with the same energy and enterprise. When we had filled the hold of the vessel with blubber - before beginning the process of 'making off,' our Captain gave us all a grand treat or feast on board. Then all was stowed away and we were to set sail on our homeward-bound voyage.

I take it now as a happy circumstance that we had not one mishap on board our lonely vessel, but through the providence and goodness of God we weathered all storms, and arrived in the Thames as well as when we left it.

When we landed, I received letters from my friends, and a handsome present from my uncle. I received a hearty farewell from every honest man on board, and as we were to part, not knowing whether we should ever sail together again - tears were shed, and even then I had to bear up more heartily the hearts of some seemingly stubborn old harpooners, and none more than my patron sailor, old John Crocket.

I wrote a letter to my sister Margaret, and enclosed one for Mrs. Sealey. It was a laconic one, because I was hoping to see them so soon. I was promising myself the pleasure of conveying to them some of my wonders of the South Pole. I had the albatross skin stuffed, and to be ready as soon as possible for presentation. The day of parting with the Captain came, and parting is unpleasant at anytime, but especially with those we respect.

"Goodbye, Tom Pill," said old Jack Crocket, "Goodbye master. You are bound, I suppose, to a friendly port. I am going to ask you a question; you will say it is a rum one, though.   I hope you will not be angry with an old mess-mate.   I've a notion you are not much of a sailor after all.   I've a strange notion coming across my mind that you are fitted for a different kind of service than whale fishing.   Do you intend to go to sea again?"

"Jack, I cannot tell you.   But for you I should not have acquitted myself as well as I have done.   I own you have been a good friend to me.   For when I was weakest, then I felt your aid.   I owe my life to your courage and should you ever come out of Hampshire, you will always hear of my whereabouts if you visit Stowmarket, or that part of Suffolk; so, farewell."

"God Bless you master, goodbye!   And if you should go to sea again, then John Crocket goes with you if he can."

And so we parted. Captain Moon rewarded us all. My uncle was highly pleased with the expedition and with his nephew, and I revisited with joy the county of Suffolk, the land of my nativity.

Chapter 9 ~ To India

No man can tell the delight of visiting the dear friends of his youth after a long separation, but those who have experienced it. Shut up in the body of a whaler, and bound upon a long voyage, and in the midst of dangers, not only of winds and waves, it may readily be supposed that our hearts could not be insensible to the most grateful feelings towards God and man, when we found ourselves restored once more to family and friends.

I spent some months at home with my friends. My uncle was pleased with me; my father and mother were proud of me, though they did not say so; for in that little society in which they moved, I was like the monkey who had seen the world. Vain, conceited young man as I was, I fancied likewise that I knew the world. I knew nothing, and had everything to learn, though I jabbered away in the buoyancy of youth, as if I could teach all who came within reach of my voice.

I dived into the past, revisited Walsham-in-the-Willows, and sat down in the very lane where those who loved me in the day of my wild run away received and gave me food and lodging more freely than any great house would give me now.

Poor Mog! Poor Gibson! Ah, I visited for, and had the pleasure of seeing you.

Mog was grown quite a matronly woman. Such an active, cleanly, comfortable person; her house so neat, her children so lovely, and her sanded brick floor so tidy, that I positively did not like to disturb with my feet the little parlour into which I was shown.

"Pray come in, sir! Pray come in! Do not be afraid; you will do me no hurt. I love to look at you, and so will my husband when he comes home to dinner. You must stop and dine with us. My husband will be so disappointed if you do not. Our fare is homely, but you will not despise it."

I never saw more perfect confidence between man and wife. Sealey had not said in vain before God and man - "with my body I thee worship, and with all my worldly goods I thee endow." He brought all his worldly goods to his wife; that wife, like an honest woman as she was, squandered nothing, provided a comfortable home and was the admiration of those who knew her. Had I been in their station of life, I never saw a couple I would more gladly have imitated.

I shall not stop to describe our homely dinner strictly - 'a toad in a hole' - but some may not know what that is; it is simply a piece of meat baked in batter, and a precious good dinner it was.

This was a very pleasant visit; and the interest these poor people took in my narrative of the adventure, made me think even then of the pleasure to be derived from the descriptive powers of the mind, especially where the information is correct and the heart thoughtful.

After having spent several months among my friends, a cadetship on the Madras establishment was offered to me, and I thought again of my position. What now must I become? I had been assistant surgeon, though nominally second mate, on board a whaler; now I was to embark for India, as one of the servants of my king and country, though in the pay of the East India Company.

According to the Alumni Cantabrigiensis, Steggall became an Ensign with the 15th Regiment Madras Native Infantry in 1810. This fits with the following reference relating to his uncle at Walsham helping to kit him out for the trip. His uncle, the Rev. John Heigham died soon after in 1812, leaving a small inheritance to 'his favourite nephew' at the age of 21.

Accordingly after taking leave of my uncle (who assisted me with an outfit), and of father, and mother, and friends, I again embarked on the wide ocean for a far distant land. Our ship was the David Scott, a fine East Indiaman, of twelve hundred tons, and a capital sea ship she was. Our commander was Captain Lock, and as we had three hundred troops on board, he had to be a captain and commander, who knew that England expected every man to do his duty; and to our respective duties he kept us all. Being a passenger merely to some future duty, my work was to look on; and the captain was much pleased with me at various times, when I lent a helping hand in a stiff breeze.

Remarkably, we came across this picture of the *'David Scott'*, which as Steggall says had a chartered tonnage of 1200 tons and was 134 feet in length. Steggall may have felt she was *'a capital sea-ship'*; other contemporary accounts describe her as being *'like a log in the water.'*

"I perceive, young man," he said to me, "that you have been on board ship before now: what part of the world have you been in?"

"I was assistant surgeon on board the Adventure, a South-Sea whaler."

"Hah, indeed! Then you must have had to rough it, and so must we."

He had scarcely said these words before the cry came "Strange ship on our lee!"

The Captain's glass was soon upon her.

"French privateer! Up with all sails."

It was now an exciting scene to us all on board. A French privateer in full sail had us evidently in sight, and in their eyes, we were a rich prize.

Now came thoughts of capture and a French prison. Napoleon had frigates cutting up our trade, and as the seas were full of our ships, and we ourselves without any convoy, we were the very prey most likely to fall beneath their guns.

I had reason to remember the terror of Napoleon's name, though I had no fear, nor the slightest intention to flinch from my duty. We were in an isolated Indiaman; but we carried with us twenty guns, and the frigate pursuing us had fifty. We were all in the same ship resolved that no French frigate should take any of us alive whilst we could stand to our guns, and as we had three hundred soldiers on board, we could show some force to meet our adversary. Let her come to close quarters if she dare! We sailed well but the Frenchman sailed faster than we did, so we had to count of his coming. He soon came within range, and fired a bad broadside at us, not one shot doing us any material damage.

We answered with far better mark, banging in two of her guns, which never made another shot. Again they sent at us, and again we sent at them; but they seemed determined to come alongside us and board us. And now our captain's judgement was seen, for not wishing to have a close broadside of thunder which might be destructive to our troops on board, he had them all on deck, with their muskets in their hands, prepared to show their teeth.

The Frenchmen no sooner saw this, than recognising us as a troop ship, they thought it best to take a tack and steer away. I was very glad when they did so, leaving us to pursue our way in peace, with only one man wounded and a few splinters in our hull.

There are plenty of accounts of French Privateers attacking poorly defended East Indiamen. As time went on, they carried more cannon and often travelled in convoy.

We gave three hearty cheers as she left us, and I confess I felt a thankfulness of spirit, something like that which I imagine a poor rabbit may feel when it escapes the danger of the polecat's gripe.

We were next day off the Cape de Verd islands, and stopped at St. Iago to take in water, which process afforded us an opportunity, who were passengers, to go ashore, and also to indulge in fresh food.

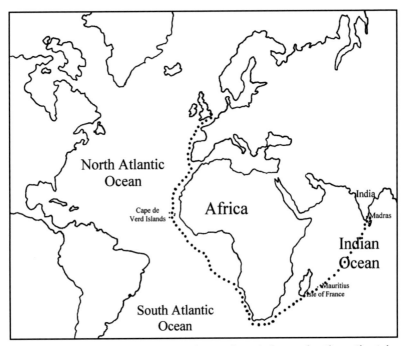

North Atlantic
Ocean

Cape de
Verd Islands

Africa

India

Madras

Indian
Ocean

Mauritius
Isle of France

South Atlantic
Ocean

We were preparing on board to take a bathe, that is four cadets, myself being one of them, had got into a boat placed alongside the vessel for that purpose. The sea was calm, an inviting ripple just moving upon the waters - the sun burning our skin, and the green waves looking delightfully cool to our heated blood. We were in the joy of youth, when sinews are strong, courage is high, and our ideas of such an enjoyment were at the summit of anticipation, when an old sailor, with his weather-beaten brow, looking over the gangway, like Palinurus, the famous pilot of old, in a gruff voice said to us -

"I say, young lads, have you any regard for the voice of an old sailor? Because if you have, well - if you have not, woe betide you."

"Why so, Jack Tar?" said one of them; "Are there any sharks in view?"

"No, boys, no. I do not mean to terrify you with sharks, but these waters are infested with something more sharp and certain than even sharks' teeth."

"What is it?"

"What is it - why certain death to you all, that's what I say, and if you like to run the risk of fever - do!"

'Fever,' thought I, 'and what fever can come from going into the water if we do not stay in too long?'

So over we all four went, and swam around the ship laughing at old Palinurus's warning, who only shook his head and said in a gruff voice, "You are four fools, and you'll all know about it."

We thought ourselves safe, and even old Palinurus was taunted for his advice. "Well shipmate," I said to him, after we had left the island about a fortnight, "and what hurt have we any of us taken?"

"Say that to me tomorrow, young ones, if you can. It is now the fourteenth day, tomorrow is the fifteenth, and if you escape, then I shall be surprised. I never knew a young lad able to bath in those waters without being dangerously ill. Your constitution yet unsettled, your blood yet boiling in your veins, you will see tomorrow, you will all of you be sick."

It was so indeed. I was the first, and all the rest soon after, as if we had been poisoned. Our heads were swollen, and our bodies covered with boils. For myself, as I knew pretty well the nature of the disease, and how difficult it was to treat it successfully, without fresh air and fresh food, without land treatment, I expected to die.

Two of my lively companions died. The shock was felt by me severely, and it had a most salutary effect upon my mind ever after. Indeed, I look back upon that time as a wonderful mercy.

One of my brother cadets and myself recovered; and as we sometimes walked the deck together, we conversed seriously upon our recent escape from the jaws of death. It was pleasant to us to receive the hearty congratulations of our fellow shipmen upon our escape, and we were both of us very penitential towards old Palinurus, who had warned us of our danger; and we became more and more thoughtful of life ever after.

It is hard to believe that the waters off a group of Atlantic Islands would have been polluted. Also, it is strange that all four of them should have been affected simultaneously. The incubation period of 15 days and the seriousness of this mysterious disease do not entirely match the consequences and known tropical diseases. It has been suggested that John Steggall is writing allegorically and is seeking to conceal the true nature of his affliction. 'We were in the joy of youth when sinews are strong... your constitution yet unsettled, your blood yet boiling in your veins... Youth was then with me, and I saw not certainly the dangers and temptations of a blindness which the rebukes of after life alone have corrected.' We are are advised by medical opinion that he may simply be alluding to a dose of syphillis and all the talk of Palinurus and the unfortunate swim are but a fable.

We did not perfectly recover from our attack all the time we were in the ship; but like two poor sickly chickens in a farmyard, we moved about without that life and spirit we used to have.

We arrived, but invalids, in the Madras Roads, and had to be taken on shore in the boats of the country, which are the only ones fit to surmount the surging breakers which surround the coast. All that day nothing could equal the kindness and hospitality of the natives and settlers of the various establishments to the European officers who came with or without recommendations, if they did but bear the characters of gentlemen.

I was received into a most friendly family house, that of a Mr. And Mrs. Irwan, under whose care I quickly recovered my wonted health. I soon received my commission as ensign of the 15th Regiment of Native Infantry. And now began my military career.

It is easy to see why a young man *'with the blood boiling in his veins'* should have chosen to go to India at this time. The old adventurers and fortune-hunters had acquired a particular eminence. Rewards and promotion within the East India Company's military section were renowned. The Company's army officers were among the best paid of their day.

I have no marvels of bloodshed to tell of. Indeed, whilst in India I was in no action whatever, for I never was fit for it. Though all the officers were kind to me, yet they saw in me very soon one that could never stand the climate of the country. They did not tell me so, but every parade day found me, though with spirit to do my duty, yet with such debility that more than once I had to be carried out of the field into the barracks. They loved and respected me for my cheerful and soldier-like deportment, but the surgeon told me I was afflicted with an enlarged liver, and I should certainly die if I staid in the country.

We are encouraged by his account of this part of the story. After all, here would be the perfect opportunity to romanticise the reality. Instead, it seems we are being given the facts alone, as he remembers them.

The symptoms that now follow, leading to his being invalided home, may be as a result of the condition he developed on the way to India. It is unclear whether they are or whether he had other problems. He makes no further mention in the book of recurrences.

It was long a question with me as to whether I ought to die or to return. So I obtained a sick certificate and went on board the Ann and sailed again for old England.

I returned with several sick passengers. The vessel had been in the merchant service, but was employed as a cruiser to protect the coasting trade in the Indian Seas. She was now sent home with despatches and sick troops. Little did I know what I yet had to suffer.

'*Ships at Anchor*' by Daniel Wright

> Lloyds Register records a ship called the *'Ann'* being built, using Teak, in Bombay in 1812. This again suggests much of this story is a year or so out, especially if the Ann was first used in the merchant service, as Steggall tells us. All in all, it is more than likely Steggall returned to England in 1812.

When we were in the Mauritius, Admiral Uvedale, as the commander then off the Isle of France, ordered us to assist in the taking of the island, and as we had many troops returning invalided or upon furlough, we formed such an addition as aided successfully in the retaking of the island, after which we sailed for England; but I was now an additional sufferer, for though not able to go ashore, we yet had to silence some forts, and received two or three sharp shots in our hull, one of which sent a splinter into my thigh, and occasioned me great agony for the rest of the voyage. But this splinter occasioned me to be honourably received at home, for now I was a wounded soldier, and had full pay, and leave of absence for three years.

An old East-Indiaman

Chapter 10 ~ The Change

It was during those three years that my mind underwent a serious change. I had seen something of the wide wide world, and being of a very reflective and thoughtful turn of mind, I became more and more seriously disposed.

This led to reading and reflection, and ultimately to such a change of occupation as to be important to me to the end of my days. I thought seriously of resigning my commission and entering the church.

According to Steggall's Cambridge University details, he was invalided home in 1811, though we have shown this was more likely to have been early in 1812. As his uncle, Rev. John Heigham died in December 1812, his decision must have been made by then. As to resigning his commission, that may not have been as easy as he thought. He had three years pension to enable him to return and by 1815 was officially absent without leave. However, priests were rarely court-martialled and he was 'struck off' the army lists in 1816. (Boase: Modern English Biography) He appears to have returned to his studies to enable himself to obtain the necessary entrance qualifications, and matriculated at Michaelmas 1813. He did not study at his father's college of St. John's, but went instead to Corpus Christi, where he was ordained as a deacon in June 1814 (Diocese of Norwich) and as a priest the following year.

The inheritance he had following his uncle's death along with his army pension probably paid for his studies, which would not have come cheaply. He speaks on the next page of the scarcity of educated men then entering the ministry. Several reports in the early nineteenth century show how true this was. As the population grew, the Anglican church found it desperately needed to recruit additional clergy, usually from the younger sons of upper class families.

My old uncle smiled at my change, but he could never defeat my arguments.   I had no wish to be a recluse, to shut myself out from the society of my fellow creatures, but I had a desire to be a clergyman.

As there was a scarcity of educated men in that day to fill the office of the ministry, and actually men were required who had a little knowledge of letters and history, as well as of mankind, and as I had not so totally forgotten all I had learnt under the Reverend William Hepworth at Botesdale School, and was not deficient in common speech or address, I had the vanity to hope that I might attain a position of usefulness and prominence in the church.   Friends I had, or I could never have gone through the necessary steps for the attainment of my object.   Those friends, too, had delicacy of feeling for me, and sent me as a fellow commoner to Corpus Christi College, Cambridge.

Corpus Christi

My object was to qualify myself to pass the necessary examination in classical and theological knowledge to

138

gain admission into the church. It was vain for me to attempt distinction at the University. I had let slip the opportunity of study which qualifies men to offer themselves for honours. It was enough for me to study sufficiently, so as to fit myself for the degree, and then to offer myself as a candidate for the ministry before the Bishop of Norwich.

There were three ranks of entering students. The first rank was Fellow Commoner, which meant an undergraduate with enough money to sit at High Table with the College Fellows. Below this were the Pensioners whose fees were privately paid. The third rank was Sizar, whereby such undergraduates obtained a kind of scholarship, but often worked as a college servant to repay some of the money.

John Steggall says he was a Fellow-Commoner, and this may ultimately have been the case, but his college record shows he was admitted as a Pensioner in June 1813.

What a different life I now had at the University. Shut out from the busy scenes of life, no more a rover over the deep, my mind turned from the mighty campaigns of Wellington, or the thundering guns of Nelson, to the study of the scriptures.

Here is an indication of how time has distorted his memory somewhat. Wellington's campaigns were very much of that time, but Nelson had been dead for nearly ten years.

I had some little difficulty in reviving my Latin and Greek from the long dormant corners of memory, but this I can say with all honour towards the fellows of my college, being men of liberality and intelligence, they received me not only with politeness, but showed themselves ready to lend a helping hand to a student like myself, entering their society late in life, and as a sailor and a soldier, a bit of a doctor, and formally a gipsy who

was now placed among them and wore a gown, or garb of distinction, which my age, more than my money, qualified me to wear.

My acquirements at the University were of a very varied nature; for though I studied divinity, I yet found in that seat of learning many pursuits congenial to a generally inquisitive mind. In due time I presented myself before the Venerable Bishop Bathurst, and was ordained. I had various curacies in his diocese. I have never been otherwise than a curate, and am now approaching three score years and ten; and singularly enough, I am at this time doing duty in that diocese, and beneath the very roof where I was best educated.

One's first curacy is always something stirring. After many years of laborious study, a minister of the Church of England has, perhaps, to take up his abode in a solitary lodging in some village. Some of the greatest divines and the most learned scholars have been so treated.

I was blest with an intelligent, pious and learned man for my rector; a man who never refused to receive me at any hour; and though afflicted with a disease in the chest, which incapacitated him from the exertion of much public speaking, yet he ever aided me and encouraged me in the discharge of my duty.

Having been once an assistant surgeon, there were many little opportunities afforded me of making myself useful to poor families, but never to the disparagement of that holy religion which it is our glory to maintain. Oh, many did I see whose poverty was their misfortune, and not arising from any want of industry either. The poor curate had to visit in distress, to minister the word of comfort, to bind up the wounds of broken limbs and broken hearts, and to share in the deepest sorrows, because he himself likewise was conscious that he was poor.

There are very few variations in a poor curate's life, especially where his daily duties are regularly performed, and his time is divided between reading and visiting the sick.

> The editing of John Steggall's story has required fairly drastic pruning of his text, even to removing whole chapters. Lengthy pieces left out are generally of a religious nature. We would strongly recommend those interested to seek out and read Steggall's complete book, but feel confident this remarkable story has not been compromised in any way by our précis.
>
> Steggall goes on at some length about his poverty, and by comparison with his father and grandfather, as a curate, rather than a rector he was certainly a lot worse off.

I was staying with an uncle at the seaside. He was a farmer in the parish of Hollesley near Woodbridge, in the County of Suffolk. It is a wild, wide-open country, and the shingly beach upon the shore has a range of Martello towers raised in the time of the threatened invasion of Napoleon the first. I love to behold the ocean and I never walk by the shore without remembering the mercies of God to me when I was myself upon the broad sea.

It was with various conversations with my Uncle that the happy hours of my visit to the seaside passed away, and it was soon after this that an even more eventful matter, as concerning my future comfort and anxiety took place; for it was my lot to meet, at my brother-in-law's house at Botesdale, a lady who in every respect was adapted to make me an excellent wife. It happened in that day, as will happen to the end of the world, that people do meet who fancy they could be happy with each other for life.

John Steggall married Sarah Weeding at Great Glemham in October 1815. He goes out of his way to tell us what a happy marriage it was. However, it has taken him till page 298 of a 320 page book to mention his wife. He says she suffered from sickness. In an application to live outside his parish (Great Ashfield) in 1831, he quotes his wife's illness as his reason for wishing to do so. For all this, she lived into her eighties. They never had any children. Sarah Steggall died in 1876. Shortly after, he married his housekeeper, Elizabeth Syer.

It had often been my privilege to meet with many agreeable ladies, but not before, to feel interested in one whom I wished to share my humble lot through life, until I met her.

My wife and I have known many privations - we have known many mercies; and I speak it with resignation, that only in the cases of sickness, which we could not avoid, and in some cases of mistaken imprudence on my part - which I shall not hesitate to declare, and in which my poor wife has been the deepest sufferer - have we known what it is to be unhappy. We have never aspired to be great people, or to live beyond our means, or attempted to launch out into anything of luxury, because we could never afford it.

We did not forget to invite Mog and her husband to come and see us.

Here is a further reminder that, unless Steggall has his dates wrong, Tom Seely was still alive in 1815. It seems likely he was the one who died, leaving a will in 1823, with property in Finningham.

The day they came, I had been taking a walk far into the country, and as I returned home, I passed a farm-house whence I saw a woman run screaming from the door, and her husband after her with a broomstick in his hand, with which he most unmercifully belaboured the poor woman's back, and knocked her down. I was a young married man at that time, and certainly had high notions of domestic kindness towards the partner of my days, and my blood boiled within me at the sight of a helpless female thus unmercifully treated by a man who looked big enough to fell an ox. I acted, perhaps, rather too impulsively, for I did not wait to argue with the man upon the occasion. I knew nothing of the nature of the provocation given him. I saw only a prostrate woman most shamefully beaten with a broomstick. I leapt over the little low paling in the front of the farmhouse, on to the grass plot where the transaction was taking place, and with the activity of a sailor, and the energy of a man of spirit, I tript up the heavy farmer who fell down upon his back; and when my spirit was up I did not stop there, for I took the broomstick and belaboured his fat sides most heartily, asking him at the same time how he liked it.

He was cowed; but not so his most obedient loving wife, for her blood was up in the cause of her husband, and I thought she would have broken my neck. She gave me such a chuck, that in one instance I dropt the broom, and, but for the lady herself into whose arms I fell backwards, I might have broken my neck in the fall. I bolted from her, seized my hat, jumping over the paling and saying, "Goodbye ye loving couple, Goodbye," I scampered off as soon as I could, laughing at my own folly, and resolving never again to interfere between man and wife, but to let them settle their own disputes.

You may suppose that Mog and my Sarah were not a little interested with this tale.

Sarah Weeding came from a family in which surgeons were prominent. Her brother was a leading Woodbridge surgeon and her sister Mary was married to John Cockle, surgeon at Trimley. We are indebted to Jean Wallwork for her research into the Weeding family wills which seem to indicate Steggall was not held in high esteem by his wife's family who made a number of references to Sarah's inheritances being for her use only and... "not be subject to the intermeddling, debts, power or control of her present or any future husband." It is interesting to note that she died before he did, but at his death he left less than two hundred pounds.

We lived in the parsonage house at Badingham, the rector having another piece of preferment at Ellough in Norfolk where he resided. The first year of my matrimonial existence, cheered and comforted as it was, by the kindest attentions of friends, rich as well as poor, convinced me that there were many good-hearted people in the world, who still participated in the happiness of others.

144

Interestingly, we have encountered evidence of John Steggall's activities at Badingham. He clearly enjoyed the role of country parson. He applied for a game certificate in October 1816 and put an advert in the Ipswich Journal in January of that year to announce: STOLEN OR STRAYED - an old Russian Pointer answers to the name of Don - reward offered 20 shillings.

Scarcely, however, had my first year of married life passed away, before a double affliction fell upon me. My father, who was rector of Wyverstone and Westhorpe, was smitten with a stroke of paralysis, and was recommended to remove to Bury St. Edmund's for medical treatment.

My sister Margaret accompanied him, and my dear wife and I had to remove to the parsonage at Wyverstone.

My poor father - liberal, kind, and considerate - had been a hard-working minister and a labouring pastor, and having no other property than his living, was compelled to sell it for the benefit of his family. I had to be his curate and to discharge the duty of family provider out of the

Hodskinson's map of Suffolk of 1783 identifies this as the Wyverstone parsonage John Steggall would have known as home. Built in the shape of a cross, it seems very small for such a family.

means then placed in my hands. The two livings were purchased by two clergymen, both of whom, like my father before them, have since been compelled to part with them. Indeed, I have lived to see them change hands twice, whilst I have had to struggle on to be the poor old curate, and to write this narrative.

This event had a profound effect on John Steggall's life. As the only clergyman son, he could have expected to enjoy the benefits of a rectorship. Charles Steggall had his stroke in 1816 just before his wife's death and needed expensive care for over three years. Added to this, John's elder brother, William Charles, an army officer, demanded his share of what remained of his father's inheritance, and the living was sold, leaving John Heigham Steggall without a parish of his own.

It was not the only affliction attendant upon my lot, for the very sudden change of affairs either increasing the energies or responsibilities of my dear partner's position, superinduced a debility of constitution, which impeded the powers of her otherwise actively disposed body and mind, and she, who was the life and assistance of my curate's home, became now my continual anxiety.

'The Curate's lot' by A. Tindal Hart describes how lowly was the lot of the poor nineteenth century parish curate, who was often the butt of contempt, ridicule or pity. Those without hope of an advowson were condemned to a life of relative poverty, occupying a parish without the tythes to fund a rectory or doing the work of an absent rector without ever reaping the reward.

My dear father was four years afflicted with paralysis, during which time he required all the attention of my sister Margaret, and all the assistance we could render him, but he died; and oh that I could pay the tribute of respect I ought to do to his memory.

I buried my poor father and now found myself a curate under one of those rectors who had been presented to the advowson by gift. The little property of that parent, after all his funeral expenses were paid, proved indeed that his treasures were not laid up upon this earth. From six hundred a year to sixty pounds per annum, is rather a sudden descent in the scale of human affairs.

A cluster of Steggall graves in the corner of Wyverstone churchyard

There were friends who felt that our circumstances, being greatly altered, were worthy of their commiseration, and this commiseration was shown in that polite withdrawal of themselves from our society, which gradually dwindled into acquaintance, and from acquaintance into total absence, and from absence into indifference, and thence into forgetfulness, until the old adage was proved, that the rich have many friends, but the poor is despised even of his own neighbour.

But another blow soon after followed, and that was certainly a severe one. The benevolent rector, Mr. R____, whose curate I was in my poor father's place, was taken away, and a man of fortune as well as a clergyman came to reside, built a new parsonage, established new schools, and became an increased blessing to the parish, though I found it injurious to my position. I have lived to see the Reverend Mr. W_____ succeeded by the Reverend Mr. C_____, and death has already laid his hand upon two rectors of that parish in the life time of the poor curate, the son of the former rector. But the savor of good men lives after them, and both Mr. R_____ and Mr. W_____ have left memorials of their benevolence and Christian charity, which live beyond the grave.

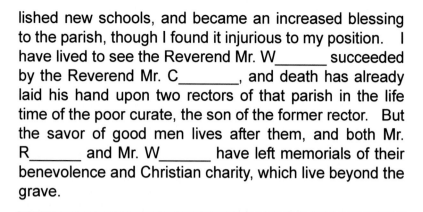

The Rectors of Wyverstone - Why Steggall persists in his not naming people when he only wishes to speak good of them is hard to understand. It merely seems to have been the fashion to write names in this way. They must all have been well known at the time, and are easily discernable from the records.
Rev. Orbel Ray, died 1829, aged 82, buried Tostock
Rev. James Ware, died 1855, aged 64, buried Wyverstone
Rev. Thomas Clarkson, died 1882, aged 69, bur. Wyverstone

I had hitherto made myself useful in a way to many poor people, having been brought up a surgeon, and having practised in various branches of the medical profession, I had also been fond of the study of the human frame, and had kept up my reading upon anatomy and the medical sciences. Serious thoughts came over my mind as to practising the medical profession in conjunction with my ministerial duties.

I had no preferment in the church except a perpetual curacy. I occasionally assisted in the discharge of duties for brother clergymen: but I found that my dear partner was suffering, and as much felt the want of active employment for me as for herself. What thought I, would be the inconsistency of my practising surgery? I knew some clergymen who were engaged as physicians, aye, and eminent ones too.   Why should I neglect the art of healing, of which I had acquired considerable knowledge in my youth?   It is not beneath any man to try and earn his bread if he can, at any time, provided he does not act dishonestly therein.   I was a clergyman, but I had no employment just at that time in that profession.

I had ability - I had activity.   My brother-in-law was a medical man, and had received assistance from me in his profession.   These things dwelt upon my mind and made me desirous of active exertion; so I resolved to set up practice as a surgeon.   I went and lived at Rattlesden, where my fame as a practitioner increased and I began to feel an independence arising from my own exertions.

John Steggall's Rattlesden practice was in this building, that has been reduced to one storey. It stands beside what is now the Brewers Arms.

A poor medical man has hacking work, but, if a steady quiet practitioner, he may get on so as to gain independence, but he must look for it among those who can pay for it - and they must have very often a deal of faith in man, and be themselves very ignorant, very patient and very poor creatures to depend so much on human skill.

I was getting up by degrees in my practice, when my

name was mentioned to the late Lord Thurlow, my noble patron, a man whose memory, as well as that of his present son, I shall ever hold in the deepest respect. That good man had but one living in his gift - and that was not a rectory, not a vicarage - but only a poor perpetual curacy. Nevertheless, that, augmented by Queen Anne's Bounty, amounting to sixty pounds per annum, that nobleman presented to me.

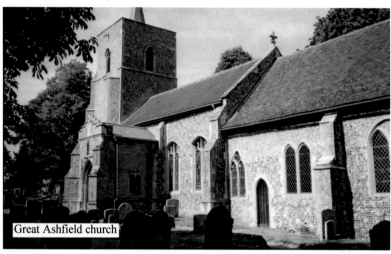
Great Ashfield church

As there was no glebe house upon the curacy, my residence was not required, so that I could still keep up my medical practice, and yet perform the stated duties of the curacy of Great Ashfield, in the county of Suffolk.

I found in Lord Thurlow an intelligent and liberal-minded friend, who, comprehending the struggles I had to maintain myself, met them with every encouragement he could give me. It was through his kindness and liberality that I was enabled to go to London, and make myself master of one branch of my medical profession, midwifery; in which I felt my deficiency, and without which, in many cases, I found I could not practise as I ought. Accordingly, I attended the course of lectures necessary to obtain the medical certificate as to my proficiency.

Though there must be some doubt as to the extent of Steggall's original apprenticeship, he did at this point obtain the formal qualification he describes. Thanks to the research of Jean Wallwork and Dr. Anita Burny, we are able to confirm that documentation shows John Steggall obtained his licentiateship of the Society of Apothecaries on Feb 1st 1827.

Lord Thurlow himself saw no impropriety in my endeavour to perfect myself for country practice, and yet he often used to wish that I could entirely devote myself to the one profession.

For a number of years J.H. Steggall must have divided his time between his patients and his parishioners, no doubt riding scores of miles a week between the villages of Rattlesden and Great Ashfield.

He asked one day plainly whether, if Great Ashfield were sufficiently endowed, I would give up my medical practice. I had no hesitation in declaring that I would, or, at least confine it to its charitable exercise for the benefit of the poor.

His lordship seemed to weigh these matters well in his mind. There was a lectureship in the same parish, instituted by one Nicholas Tyrmage, who left three hundred to be invested in the year 1620, for a preaching minister of God's word who was to preach every Sunday in the forenoon in that parish church.

This money was invested in the purchase of about forty acres of land, called Hoo Wood in Stowupland and Stowmarket. Land in Hackford was also left for the same purpose, and the rents amounted to about £98 per annum.

The property was placed in the hands of trustees, who, up to the year 1813, used to appoint the curate to the lectureship; but after that year they began to appoint some other clergyman.

Lord Thurlow thought this a question that ought to be decided by the law, for it was evidently a detriment to the preferment that the parochial minister should not have the advantage of the bequest intended for him. His Lordship thought it a stretch of authority in the trustees to give it to another and wished me to try the question. As he was patron, and interested therein, he promised to see me harmless in the expense.

The lectureship - This was a prolonged legal battle the details of which are to be found in a number of places. White's directory for Suffolk, 1844, describes how the then lecturer, Rev. T. B. Norgate was in 1827 prohibited from performing duty in the church. It is interesting to note that John Heigham Steggall from 1830, until he loses the case in January 1833, signs the parish register as *'Curate and Lecturer.'* He was clearly confident of winning.

Ironically, he finally claimed the lectureship towards the end of his life in 1876, at a time when his health was failing and he was probably incapable of fulfilling the demands of the post.

It was in consequence of this, and from no private malice, that an action at law was commenced by me, and all the question turned upon the point between the article 'the,' and 'a.' The words were not specifically, "The preaching minister of the gospel," but "a preaching minister"; so that, as the deed did not state who that was to be, the trustees were confirmed in their judgement, and I lost my cause.

One affliction seldom comes alone. There generally follows another in quick succession, to remind us all that it is a bitter, though a wholesome cup we have to drink. I was made to feel most deeply the loss of that inestimable nobleman, the late Lord Thurlow.

The original Baron Thurlow was a remarkable man, rising from being a distinguished lawyer (in spite of never completing his degree) to becoming both Attorney-General and Lord Chancellor to George III, which led to his elevation to the peerage. His nephew Edward inherited the title in 1806. It is his death that Steggall is here describing. He was succeeded by Rt. Hon. Edward Thomas Hovell Thurlow in 1829.

He died not long after the loss of my cause concerning the augmentation of the living. I felt the loss of him more than I can express. He was almost my warm friend - always lent me the aid of counsel - and was never backward in doing good.

Great was our loss, though he was succeeded in his title and estates by a son who was even more liberal and kind to me than his father. Not only did he pay all my expenses in the law-suit for which I had no written document; in a thousand ways he has proved that the bright spirit of old England's true nobility descends with honour upon the son who imitates his father's good example.

Not long after the loss of one law suit, I found myself involved in another. I had been practising surgery, because I was originally brought up to it, and held no preferment then but the perpetual curacy, and had none to look forward to.

Why should not a clergyman, brought up practically as an assistant-surgeon, when not provided for, attempt to earn his livelihood by relieving humanity in the same laudable manner in which surgeons constantly do - it be one of the most human and useful studies to which he could devote himself.

About this time I had a patient who had an inflammation in her foot and instep, very violent, and though decidedly not of a dangerous character, yet her subsequent mistake, if not wilful, led to very serious consequences. I ordered that she should place it in warm water, not in cold. She did directly the reverse, whether from mistaking my advice, or from the natural idea of

---

This unfortunate case has already been the subject of an article by local doctor Edward Cockayne, published in the Journal of the Royal Society of Medicine (Vol. 92, Feb 1999) entitled: *'The Misfortune of John Steggall, a Country Practitioner.'*

In this piece, Ted Cockayne suggests that whilst there may have been mistakes on Steggall's part, he was a victim of bad luck and professional jealousy on the part of other local doctors whom he undercut. The case was covered by the local press and full reports appeared in the Bury Post for April 1839.

Following an exchange of letters to the Lancet and the Society of Apothecaries the previous year regarding Steggall's qualification and his cut-price fees, Dr. Bree of Stowmarket was clearly awaiting his opportunity to pounce. When the nine-year old daughter of Joseph Gladwell ended up having her leg amputated, several eminent local practitioners lined up to condemn John Steggall. He lost the case and was fined £10, a substantial amount for such a case at that time. Though he was not officially 'struck off' as such, a more traditional means was employed to put an end to his practice - the hue and cry. Effectively it was the end of his career as a surgeon and he would be forced to fall back on his meagre income as a curate.

cooling her leg, I could not tell. She did not follow my advice, to a certainty. She placed her foot in cold water; mortification came on rapidly and frightfully. Another medical man was called in; the case became exaggerated; the limb was amputated, and the woman was recommended to bring an action against me for the loss of her leg. Heavy damages were sought for.

She obtained a verdict for ten pounds damages, and, of course, a hue and cry was raised against me, though I was acknowledged to be a regularly educated practitioner. I say nothing against surgeons. I know all the jealousies of the profession. I well know the hacking work they have, and the responsibility attached to the exercise of their profession. I know, moreover, there are some of the noblest and best of men, morally speaking, among them. But I know that if it were not for the very fearful amount of ignorance, and the dependence which ignorant people place upon them, their profession would not be as good as it is.

Had I been a surgeon only, I might not have been persecuted on account of the unfortunate case alluded to; but I happened to be a poorly-paid and half-employed clergyman. Also I soon found that it was useless to attempt to carry on my practice.

Steggall appears to have abandoned the Rattlesden property where he once operated as a surgeon. However, he continued to live for a short time just across the parish boundary in Drinkstone where in 1841, he is recorded as paying tithes. He continued to own and let this house for some time after moving to Great Ashfield. An agreement survives from 1851 that shows Charles Cooper paid £13 per annum for rent on the house, stables, chaise-house, other outbuildings and an acre of land.

Never shall I forget the kindness of the present Lord Thurlow. It was noble. He proposed that I should come and reside in the parish of Great Ashfield, and live among my people. He not only made the proposition, but, to his honour, he built for me, at his own expense, the nice substantial parsonage house in which I now reside. It cost him a considerable sum, and it exhibits the taste, as well as the generosity, of the nobleman. No man was more active, or more desirous of doing good to others than the present Lord Thurlow. I speak with a grateful heart from experience, and I am sure that others, if they had the opportunity, would speak it as publicly as I do.

Lord Thurlow built us a house, and thanks to his Lordship it is one both durable, convenient and substantial, and will stand for generations, when I, the poor old curate, am no more.

The Parsonage at Great Ashfield

It may be interesting to the reader to know that I still live in the little parsonage of Great Ashfield, in the County of Suffolk, provided for me by my noble patron, and still pursue the even tenor of an old man's days. We visit our poor people and minister in a small way to their little wants.   My house stands close to the roadside, is built in the Elizabethan style, and is a great place in miniature. One dell of a meadow runs along the road by its side, and the house itself hides the little garden from the road.   My church is seen from the windows, and so are many of my poor people's cottages.   Lord Thurlow's mansion is hidden by a hill, and he himself is not resident.

I wish he was, but till he is again
God grant in health and peace he may remain;
Joy will it be whene'er that welcome day
Shall bring him back amidst us here to stay.

The Arms of The Right Honourable Thomas Edward Hovell Thurlow,
Baron Thurlow of Thurlow

After all that

The book must have been quite successful. It was published a number of times, firstly by Simpkin, Marshall & Co. and later by Ward Lock. It carried several different titles: *The Real History of a Suffolk Man, The Life of John H. Steggall* and finally, *The Suffolk Gipsy*. People we have met have a variety of editions; it was even published as a cheap early paperback, but was out of print by 1900. We have no idea how much Steggall ever made from the book, but as we have shown, he did not die a rich man. He did however die an old man, at the age of 90, having been curate at Great Ashfield for well over 50 years. In his later years, he was referred to as vicar of that parish.

Richard Cobbold spoke of John Steggall as *'a venerable old gentleman'* when he met him in 1854, yet Steggall outlived the younger Cobbold by four years. What was more, having buried his wife Sarah in 1876, Steggall married his 36 year-old housekeeper, Elizabeth Syer in 1879, when his own health must have been failing. Reports at his death suggest he had not been fit to preach for two or three years. Elizabeth Steggall inherited *'under two hundred pounds'* in her husband's will, and was later married again to a Mr. John C. Ford, Master of Bury St. Edmunds Municipal Workhouse. This time her new husband was only twenty years her senior.

As he remained so long in one place, it enables us to trace John Steggall and his household through several censuses. Like so much in history, these census details create more questions than they answer.

1841: Drinkstone

John Steggall	50	Minister
Sarah Steggall	45	
Jane Humphries	20	Servant

1851: Great Ashfield Parsonage

John Steggall MD	60	Perpetual Curate born Needham Market
Sarah Steggall (wife)	57	born Ramsholt
Mary Cockle (sister)	70	Doctor's widow born Shottisham
Selina Hubbard	16	Servant, born Badwell
Margit Rice	20	Servant, born Wolverstone

Mary Cockle was actually the sister of Sarah Steggall

1861: Great Ashfield Parsonage, Elmswell Rd.

John H. Steggall	72	Church clergyman
Sarah Steggall	60	
Thomas A. Boileau	42	Boarder - retired Capt. of the army, born in India
Rose Miller	19	Servant, born Pakenham

1871: Great Ashfield Vicarage

John H. Steggall	80	
Sarah Steggall	75	
Thomas Boileau	52	

(pensioned officer, East India British subject)

Rebecca Price	20	

(Domestic servant, born Pakenham)

Priscilla Barrell	17	

(Domestic servant, born Ashfield)

1881: Great Ashfield Vicarage

Elizabeth Steggall	40	Annuitant, born Brandon
Thomas A. Boileau	62	(British Subject) born East Indies handicap - imbecile
Mary A. Biss	62	visitor, born Middlesex
Sophia Pattle	19	Servant, born Wyverstone

160

Who was the mysterious Thomas Boileau who seems to have lived there for over 20 years. Was he a link with John Steggall's time in India? (even though he was born after Steggall came back) And when did this retired army officer become an imbecile?

Records for Wyverstone (the Steggall family parish) show that the remainder of the Rev. Charles Steggall's estate passed to John Steggall's elder brother, William Charles. This was for the most part a farmhouse and land known today as Knights Court. There he remained until his death in 1850, having served time as a Soldier with the 43rd Light Infantry. An interesting relic of his years in Wyverstone turned up in a chimney in one of a pair of cottages in Mill Road.

Beneath a stone in the chimney bearing the name of William Charles Steggall, a piece of scorched paper has been found bearing the words *'William Charles Steggall of 43rd Light Infantry Eldest Son of the Revd. Chas. Steggall 25 years Rector of this parish Aged 42 years Grandson of William Steggall 50 years Rector, Created this House & Chimney, 1819 and herewith deposits a silver coin the Value of Six pence The outer walls of this Cottage extend 40 feet in length & 13 in bredth of Clay lumps unburnt WCS render in the cottage opposite which he has recently repaired & A L Lanford & R Lanford the ground.'* You can see where the coin was once attached. A military uniform was also secreted inside the chimney.

To nail our colours to the mast, we feel there is a good deal of truth in the story of John Heigham Steggall. Much is muddled, especially his early life and it is most unlikely he was present at the shooting of the gamekeeper, though he probably heard the story round the campfire one night. Though he claims he could write volumes about his time with the gipsies, it is unclear how much time he spent hiding out with them - it could have been days, weeks or months. Whatever the truth may be, he seems to have felt a warmth and a gratitude for their help in his time of need. Almost certainly, Gibson's story is a fiction told to an impressionable child who chose to believe it. Much must have been forgotten, however, and other detail inserted, so it is hard to know what to believe.

To use the name of Tom Sealey as the gamekeeper suggests there was truth in this story. There were men known by that name living only a short distance from Steggall himself (allowing for variations in spelling). In 1827, the younger Tom Seeley, his wife Sophia and their first four children (see the family tree at the end of this book) were the subjects of a settlement order, sending them back from Norton to Finningham. Finningham, being next to Wyverstone, Steggall must have been aware all along he was using the name of a real person. But what the connection was between the Seelys and local gipsies is hard to ascertain. Both Tom Seelys on our family tree married into established local families, though in both cases, they carried a certain notoriety. The Osbornes were reputed to be witches and several Fletchers had criminal records.

Then there is the case of what else was being published at the time. George Borrow's *'Lavengro'* had made gipsies into the stuff of best sellers. There are some uncomfortable similarities between Borrow's books and *The Suffolk Gipsy.* Borrow encounters gipsies at the age of seven, though they appear much more suspicious than Steggall's gipsies. Borrow recounts also a young man being sung to by a gipsy girl. In our abbreviated version of Steggall's book, we have omitted interactions between the young curate, a Jew and an Irish Catholic. These too are themes that crop up in the works of George Borrow. We have already shown how a popular literary theme of the time, whaling, has added to the romance and excitement of the novel. But it is supposed to be more than a novel - almost an autobiography. Whether the suspected plagiarism is Steggall's or can be laid at the door of the editor, Richard Cobbold is unclear. But it does lead us to believe that, in searching for an audience, the pair of them have been prepared to exaggerate, elaborate and fill in the forgotten details as though they were fact.

For all that, we are of the opinion that this story is sub-stantially true - he did come from a family of parsons, he did run away from a school that treated boys as cruelly as those at *Dotheboys Hall.* It seems likely he did go to sea - he certainly shows good knowledge of life aboard a sailing ship - but as less than 30 ships a year sailed to the Southern Ocean in search of Whales, that may be an elaboration. The army sequence seems to fit the facts and he tells it straight and simple. After that, his Cambridge years, his work as a priest and a surgeon fit what we can show to be true, albeit through Steggall's eyes. His inability to settle to anything in his early years seems to have troubled his wife's family who were care-ful in drafting their wills. The similarity of parts of his story to those of other writers may have been as a result of reading the published works of his time and realising there was something he could write about his life that people would want to read.

Oral accounts still abound in the district that sometimes vary wildly from the published version. We found people who told us that a gamekeeper called Seely had shot a gipsy he caught poaching in Norton Wood: also that a rich Seely from the Midlands had come to East Anglia, married a gipsy and become a gamekeeper.

The main problem in researching this book has been the readiness of many writers to use Steggall's book as the one source of information when reporting on his life. It is likely, his Cambridge University biography owes much to the book. His obituary published in the Bury Free Press on January 29th 1881 was clearly compiled as a summary of the book. Articles in the East Anglian Miscellany make good use of Steggall family wills, but still rely on *'The Suffolk Gipsy'* for biographical detail. The Miscellany does give us a few interesting later facts. John Steggall, it is suggested, met his second wife buying furniture at a sale at Walsham-le-Willows and ended up having to go through the ceremony twice, because the first wedding service had been before 8 o'clock in the morning, and was found to be not legal.

Responding to the editor's request for remembrances of *'The Suffolk Gipsy'*, Charles Pettiward in 1930 still remembered him fondly as *'a pleasant old gentleman with a white beard.'*

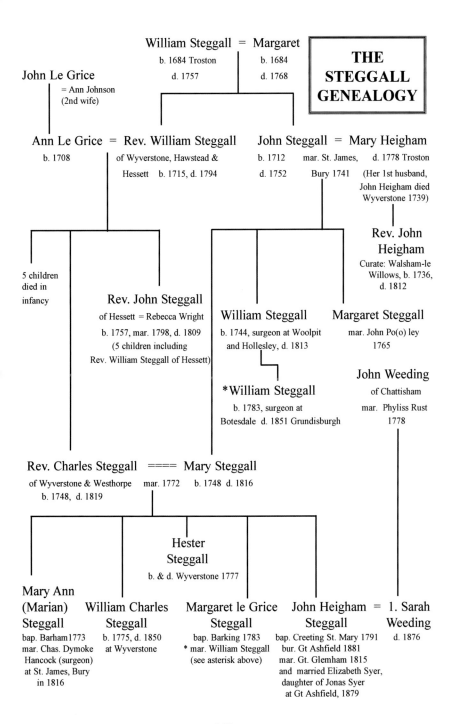

William Steggall = Margaret
b. 1684 Troston   b. 1684
d. 1757   d. 1768

THE
STEGGALL
GENEALOGY

John Le Grice
= Ann Johnson
(2nd wife)

Ann Le Grice = Rev. William Steggall
b. 1708   of Wyverstone, Hawstead &
                 Hessett b. 1715, d. 1794

John Steggall = Mary Heigham
b. 1712   mar. St. James,   d. 1778 Troston
d. 1752   Bury 1741   (Her 1st husband,
                           John Heigham died
                           Wyverstone 1739)

Rev. John
Heigham
Curate: Walsham-le
Willows, b. 1736,
d. 1812

5 children
died in
infancy

Rev. John Steggall
of Hessett = Rebecca Wright
b. 1757, mar. 1798, d. 1809
(5 children including
Rev. William Steggall of Hessett)

William Steggall
b. 1744, surgeon at Woolpit
and Hollesley, d. 1813

Margaret Steggall
mar. John Po(o)ley
1765

John Weeding
of Chattisham
mar. Phyliss Rust
1778

*William Steggall
b. 1783, surgeon at
Botesdale d. 1851 Grundisburgh

Rev. Charles Steggall ==== Mary Steggall
of Wyverstone & Westhorpe mar. 1772   b. 1748 d. 1816
b. 1748, d. 1819

Hester
Steggall
b. & d. Wyverstone 1777

Mary Ann
(Marian)
Steggall
bap. Barham1773
mar. Chas. Dymoke
Hancock (surgeon)
at St. James, Bury
in 1816

William Charles
Steggall
b. 1775, d. 1850
at Wyverstone

Margaret le Grice
Steggall
bap. Barking 1783
* mar. William Steggall
(see asterisk above)

John Heigham = 1. Sarah
Steggall   Weeding
bap. Creeting St. Mary 1791   d. 1876
bur. Gt Ashfield 1881
mar. Gt. Glemham 1815
and married Elizabeth Syer,
daughter of Jonas Syer
at Gt Ashfield, 1879

165

An attempt to construct the Seely Genealogy

(this name is spelt in a variety of ways
- Sealey, Sealy, Seely, Seeley, etc.)

Thomas Seely = Susan Osborn

married around 1781

died, either 1808	died 1826
(bur. Finningham)	(bur. Finningham)
or 1823 (left a will)	

Thomas bap. (F) 1782, bur. (F) 1792	Lydia b. around 1786 bur. 1810	Mary b. around 1792 mar. John Pope (F) 1813	Elijah b. 1796 mar. Lucy Brook Walsham 1822 lived at Norton	George b. 1801 mar. Eliz. Farrow (F) 1825

Susan bap (F) 1784 mar. Robert Lambert 1805	William bap (F) 1788 mar. Hannah Day (F) 1810 and mar. Eliz. Sear (F) 1826	Lucy b. around 1794 mar. Ed. Spink (F) 1816	Frances b. 1799

Thomas Seeley = Sophia Fletcher
(blacksmith)   mar. Norton 1817
bap. Finningham 1796

Elijah b. 1820	Henry b. 1824	Alfred b. 1829	Sophia b. 1835

Sophia b. 1818	Mahala b. 1822	Robert b. 1828	Hannah b. 1833	Sarah b.1838

All of the children of Thomas and Sophia were baptised in Finningham.
(F) means these were recorded in the Finningham register
Three of the sons of Thomas and Susan Seely were carpenters.
We have been unable to detect a gamekeeper in the family

Bibliography

Biographical list of boys educated at King Edward VI Free Grammar School, Bury St. Edmunds   Paul & Matthew 1908

Boase, F.   *Modern English Biography:* Volume 6
                            rep. Frank Cass 1965

Borrow, G.   *Lavengro: the scholar, the gypsy, the priest*
                            Dent 1906 (Borrow's books have been
                            published many times before & after)

Borrow, G.   *The Zincali, an account of the Gipsies of Spain*
                            Murray 1901

Bury Free Press   January 29th 1881

Bury Post   April 3rd 1839, April 10th 1839

Chatterton, E.Keble   *Old East Indiamen* Conway Maritime Press
1971

Cockayne, Edward MB FRCGP
                            *'The misfortune of John Steggall, a country
                            practitioner'* in Journal of the Royal Society of
                                    Medicine, Vol. 92, February 1999.

Gardner, B.   *The East India Company: A History*
                            Hart-Davis 1971

Hart, A.Tindal   *The Curate's Lot: The story of the unbeneficed*
                            J. Baker 1970

Ipswich Journal   April 12th 1788

Ipswich Journal   January 31st 1807, July 18th 1807

Jackson, G.   *The British Whaling Trade* A & C Black 1978

Kingston, H.G.   *The South Sea Whaler* (1851)

Kingston, H.G.   *Peter The Whaler* (1851)

Lee Terrence   *The Smith Gipsy genealogies and related
                            families* (privately published 1995)

Pocket Histories of Suffolk Parishes - Norton - reprinted from Suffolk
                            Chronicle 1928

Public Record Office: CUST 17: States of Navigation, Commerce and
                                    Revenue

Spence, B.   *Harpooned: The Story of Whaling*
                            Conway Maritime Press 1980

Suffolk Miscellany   Articles Numbered: 8174, 8177, 8182, 8185
                                    and 8220

Thompson, T.W.   *'Youngs, Gibsons and their associates - an
                            inquiry into the origin of certain East Anglian
                            and Metropolitian Gypsy families'*
                            Journal of the Gypsy Lore Society Vol. XXIV

Toulson S.	*East Anglia: Walking the Ley Lines*
Turner J.	Writing in the Walsham Village History Group Quarterly Review, 2003/4
Venn J.A.	*Alumni Cantabrigiensis* C.U.Press 1922
Vesey-Fitzgerald, B.	*Gypsy Borrow* Dobson 1953
Wallwork, J.	*'John. H. Steggall: A Real History of a Suffolk Man'* in 'Roots,' the Journal of the Suffolk Family History Society
Wallwork J.	*'Samuel Weeding, Surgeon'* in 'Roots,' the Journal of the Suffolk Family History Society

Other books by Pip & Joy Wright:
Newspapers in Suffolk **(6 vols.)**
Grave Reports
Witches in and around Suffolk
Diary of a Poor Suffolk Woodman **(with Léonie Robinson)**
pub. by Poppyland Publishing
Lydia
I Read it in the Local Rag
Death Recorded
Daniel Malden